231 DAYS:

A MIRACULOUS TRUE STORY OF FAITH IN THE FACE OF TERROR

By Herb and Linda Gregg
With James Kirby Martin

PastQuest Media

There is Always Hope for Miracles through Faith and Prayer

Daniel 3: 24-26

Then King Nebuchadnezzar leaped
to his feet in amazement and asked his
advisers, "Weren't there three men that we
tied up and threw into the fire?"
They replied, "Certainly, O king."
He said, "Look! I see four men walking
around in the fire, unbound and unharmed,
and the fourth looks like a son of the gods."

Daniel 6: 26-27

For He is the living God
And He endures forever;
He rescues and he saves;
He performs signs and wonders
in the heavens and on the earth.
He has rescued Daniel
from the power of the lions.

Luke 1: 37

For nothing is impossible with God

Paperback ISBN: 979-8-9878974-0-9

Cover design and layout by Lucy Holtsnider
LucyHoltsnider.com
Published in Houston, Texas, USA

Table of Contents

Herb and Linda's story takes place in the mountainous North Caucasus region that features the countries of Dagestan and Chechnya.

FOREWORD: 231 DAYS

Some stories are hard to believe. Many of these same stories are deeply inspirational. They can encourage and bolster us in our Christian walks. They can remind us that God's omnipresent power knows no bounds, that through prayer and believing we can triumph in the harrowing battles of life. With this thought, the kidnapping of Christian missionary Herb Gregg, Jr., the daily threats to his well-being that followed, and his miraculous release from captivity represent a timeless—and timely—story of faith in action when chances for survival varied between slim and none. In the end, Herb triumphed. That is the unbelievable and inspirational story that follows.

The events that took place happened in the neighboring republics of Dagestan and Chechnya in the mountainous region called the North Caucasus, just south of Russia. In 1995 Herb and his wife Linda moved to Makhachkala, the capital city of Dagestan, situated along the shoreline of the Caspian Sea. Scenically, the city has a beautiful setting lying between a glistening sea and snow-capped mountains off in the distance. However, the local population of some 250,000 people were enduring an unemployment rate of up to 80 percent. With the economy in pitiful shape, corruption, crime, and occasional outbursts of violence too often characterized the reality of street life in Makhachkala.

One might fairly ask: What were these long-serving missionaries doing in this depressed country? The Gregg's story line goes back many years—all the way back into the 1960s when they first met and found a unifying bond in their love of Jesus Christ. Together they felt a strong calling for mission work. They married in 1971 after Herb completed a two-year tour in the Marine Corps. Then he finished college at California State at Fullerton, after which he taught school for three years. In 1977, they finally realized their dream when the Church of the Redeemer in Mesa, Arizona, sponsored them to go to Brazil. There they both trained for and engaged in mission-related assignments.

Returning to Arizona in 1980, Herb and Linda made contact with TEAM—The Evangelical Alliance Mission—whose home office was in Carol Stream, Illinois, a suburb of Chicago. TEAM was regularly active (and still is) in sending resolute, diligent, Bible-believing missionaries across the globe. With financial backing from TEAM and its affiliated churches, the Greggs, having learned how to speak Portuguese in Brazil, relocated with their two children, Amy and Jason, to Portugal. There they served the Lord in various locations, including Lisbon, where they focused on church planting activities and on witnessing with great enthusiasm to potential converts about God's plan of salvation through the redeeming grace of Jesus Christ.

Ten years later, in 1991, a seismic shift in the world political order took place. The Union of Socialist Soviet Republics, the U.S.S.R., collapsed under the weight of its own inflexible political and economic rigidities. In the 1980s Russia's president, Mikhail Gorbachev (1931-2022) began to advocate greater political openness (*glasnost*) as well as reconstruction (*perestroika*) in moving away from the oppressive political and economic realities of life under the dominant, old line Communist Party.

By 1990, as part of this upheaval, various satellite Soviet republics, among them the Baltic States and Ukraine, were seeking complete independence. In response, a coup attempt by Soviet hardliners to remove Gorbachev from power failed in August 1991 but also so weakened him that removal became inevitable. On December 25, 1991, the Soviet sickle-and-hammer flag was taken down at the Kremlin and replaced by the tricolor Russian flag. Boris Yeltsin (1931-2007) replaced Gorbachev as president, and the U.S.S.R. was no more. The new political entity came to be named the Russian Federation.

One of the themes of *glasnost* was to tear down the Iron Curtain and open Soviet society to outsiders who might help improve the depressed standard of living being experienced by millions existing at or below a poverty level of life. Tangentially related were religious matters. The U.S.S.R. was an avowed atheistic nation where the life-crushing Communist dictator Joseph Stalin (1878-1953) ruled ruthlessly as a substitute for God. The Eastern Orthodox Church struggled to stay alive by avoiding challenges to the all-pervading will of the Communist Party. But now, beginning in 1992, the Curtain had been raised, and Christian missionaries would be welcome to cross over the once rigid Iron barrier and share God's Word in the newfound Soviet Federation.

Herb attended an informational meeting in France where an area TEAM director encouraged veteran missionaries to redeploy and share the Word with the unreached people of Russia. Feeling that their church plants in Portugal were now strong enough to prosper and grow on their own, the Greggs moved to Moscow in 1994. There they spent a year engaged in learning the Russian language while contemplating exactly where they should next locate in their missionary outreach activities. Even with warnings about their personal safety, they felt called to settle in Dagestan with its ethnically diverse population of around two million people, most of whom had never had any exposure to basic beliefs of the Christian faith.

Unlike the Baltic States and Ukraine and a few other former Soviet satellite republics, Dagestan after 1991 had preferred to continue its political existence as a republic operating under the umbrella of the newly founded Russian Federation. A sense of national identity prevailed in this small country, about the size of West Virginia, containing 34 distinct ethno-linguistic groups. Some 90 percent of these people were non-militant Muslims who did not favor fundamentalist Sharia law. Generally, they were tolerant of the small number of practicing Jews, about two percent of the population, living in enclaves among them. The remaining eight percent identified, at least in some nominal way, with the Eastern Orthodox Church.

Besides teaching English at Makhachkala's Pedagogical University and helping out at a local orphanage, Herb and Linda aspired to plant a Christ-centered church that would reach out to all ethnic groups in Dagestan. Over time, this new fellowship of believers would function as the seed for furthering the growth of Christianity in this isolated Russian republic. Slowly but steadily, and with the assistance of a few other TEAM helpers, this congregation began to grow and thrive, at least until the day when a local gang of Dagestanis, masking as police officers, abducted Herb and hustled him away from the streets of Makhachkala.

What had happened? Herb had become a target of one of some 70 kidnapping gangs then operating out of Chechnya, Dagestan's immediate neighbor to the west. This small republic, little more than the size of Rhode Island and noted for its breathtaking mountainous terrain, was then seeking full independence from the Russian Federation. Back in 1991, even before the final collapse of the U.S.S.R., Chechens had voted for complete separation. After much negotiation with the Boris Yeltsin regime, brutal warfare broke out in 1994. Bouts of bloody combat between Russian soldiers and Chechen partisans cost thousands of lives on both sides. Just as bad was the massive dislocation of refugees, a half million people or around 40 percent of Chechnya's population of 1.5 million, who fled their homes amid the horrible scenes of human violence.

In late 1996 Boris Yeltsin decided to end this destructive war by promising to accept Chechnya's demand for complete independence. What was left was a war-torn, poverty-stricken mess. All the fighting and the devastation of Grozny, Chechnya's capital city, left the local economy in a complete shambles. Peace time employment did not exist for hundreds upon hundreds of Chechen freedom fighters. As an alternative occupation for almost no available jobs, especially for young adult males, seizing hostages and threatening them with death—or executing them if ransoms were not paid—emerged as a highly profitable alternative form of industry. Wartime brutalities simply morphed into peacetime cruelties involving many hundreds of victims of hostage-taking, among them Herb Gregg, Jr.

Facilitating this newfound wave of human violence were some powerful warlords, such as Arbi Barayev (1974-2001), who controlled hundreds of militant followers in what functioned as his own private army.[1] Barayev was representative of those warlords who fought so determinedly to secure Chechnya's independence. They were also determined to see the fundamentalist form of their Muslim faith, known as Wahhabism, become completely dominant in the North Caucasus region.

Founded in Saudi Arabia back in the eighteenth century, Wahhabi adherents, among them power players like Barayev, were actively spreading this radical form of Muslim faith, as embodied in Sharia law, into Chechnya and even Dagestan. In the mid-1990s Wahhabism was growing daily in its influence, but as yet only represented no more than 5 percent of the population. However, Wahhabis like Barayev thought expansively. They had the goal of establishing a united, independent Muslim nation that also included Dagestan, with everyone subscribing to purist Wahhabi beliefs—freed of outside influences, including almost anything Russian and certainly, too, Christianity.

Kidnapping, of which Barayev was a well-known primary instigator—and sometime butcher—involved securing ransom money to buy more weapons and supplies in support of what seemed

---

1 Barayev organized and maintained what was known as his Special Purpose Islamic Regiment, a force of about one thousand militants who provided muscle for all sorts of criminal activities, not the least of which was kidnapping. A dangerous man with close operational ties to Osama bin Laden, Barayev emerged as a major target of Russian leaders for elimination. In 2001, he was captured and reportedly tortured to death.

like endless local warfare. After 1996 these arms in turn would be used to defeat other warlords, as well as the elected president of Chechnya, Aslan Maskhadov (1951-2005), who had wanted Chechnya to remain a more secular Muslim country. In 1998 and into 1999, an undeclared civil war between the Wahhabis and Muslim traditionalists was producing internal chaos in Chechnya. In that latter year, Maskhadov conceded to the Wahhabis and mandated Sharia law, which somewhat eased local Muslim religious tensions but did not bring an end to kidnappings.[2]

Maskhadov had acted to save his presidency, knowing that warlords like Barayev were also getting additional financial support from outside sources. Prominent among them was the very wealthy and well-known Wahhabi activist, Osama bin Laden (1957-2011), who was operating out of Saudi Arabia and Afghanistan at that time. Further, there was bin Laden's Wahhabi acolyte, Emir Khattab (1969-2002) who was adept in setting up paramilitary training camps, first in Afghanistan and by the mid-1990s in Chechnya.[3] In these camps young men and women learned to fight and kill aggressively, even if that meant sacrificing their own lives, in jihad-like actions directed against those who dared to question or doubt fundamentalist Muslim beliefs.

Why offer this background information on Chechnya? The answer is that a Chechen kidnapping gang, possibly even that of Arbi Barayev, hired a Dagestani hit squad to abduct Herb. These

---

2 President Maskhadov kept trying to rein in Barayev and other powerful warlords, but he failed to subdue them. He survived three assassination attempts and tried but failed to end all the kidnapping going on. In 1999 he took a leadership role against the Russian Federation in what became the Second Chechen War. Maskhadov died ingloriously in March 2005 when Russian Special Forces overran a military position he was defending

3 Khattab was a primary leader in organizing what came to be called the Islamic Peacekeeping Army, a Wahhabi force numbering in the hundreds that participated in an invasion of towns in northern Dagestan during August 1999. This action was the spark that ignited the Second Chechen War. The Russians managed to get a poisoned letter in Khattab's hands that killed him in March 2002.

local gangsters waylaid Herb late on the afternoon of November 11, 1998, and off they transported him to Chechnya where he would be incarcerated while enduring brutal treatment and death threats for several months. The Chechen kidnappers demanded a large ransom payment, reportedly 3.5 million U. S. dollars (well over 10 million dollars today), for his release. Not making the payment would mean some form of ghastly end to his life.

Besides wanting money, other reasons were in play for targeting Herb. His captors had no tolerance for his Christian missionary work. He was, from their perspective, a foreign infidel, no less an American whom they viewed as an unwelcome alien in their Muslim world. Since they had contempt for his Christian beliefs, some even dismissed him as a fake missionary who was really a CIA plant spying on them—and their militant faith. Like Osama bin Laden, they wanted to get rid of all foreigners in their midst, a basic step toward purifying the Chechen/Dagestan landscape of dangerous influences. Many of them also assumed that all Americans and agencies sponsoring them—in this case TEAM—would have no problem producing ransom money. And if they didn't pay, then putting this suspect Christian outsider to tortuous death would resolve the issue of his unwanted presence among them.

Whatever their thinking, receiving a huge ransom payment was their primary objective, regardless of whether Herb lived or died. The only other option, should no ransom be forthcoming, was for Herb to convert—convincingly—to Muslim Wahhabism. But Herb was deeply committed to his Christian faith, as his captors repeatedly learned, no matter what form of abuse they inflicted on him

How and why Herb survived his incarceration, and how Linda coped with the unexpected abduction of her husband are at the heart of this remarkable story. What follows is their narrative, written by them and carefully edited on their behalf by me. It's a story of frightening moments and miraculous experiences. It's a story of unwavering faith in calling upon and standing with God and his son Jesus Christ, even when Herb faced physical or bodily mutilation and constant death threats.

Stated differently, it's a story of how Herb and Linda entered the Lion's Den with Daniel and walked through burning flames with Shadrach, Meshach, and Abednego, always with their Savior rescuing them. Theirs is both an uplifting and universal story of believing faith in God as the key to overcoming man-breathed doubts and fears. Both inspirational and unforgettable, their story will encourage people everywhere to stand up and shout, as one, the magnificent news that God is ready, willing, and able to guide each of us through the travails of life as we choose to walk with Him. It's the story of the world's darkness being overcome by the brilliant light of God's greatness, as the words and actions of Herb and Linda so magnificently demonstrate in the pages ahead.

—James Kirby Martin

I

ABDUCTION

Herb

November 11–12, Makhachkala

Capital City of Dagestan by the Caspian Sea

I should have been more alert. Alka and I were having a good talk about John 3:16 and were totally engrossed in our conversation.[4] So I didn't pay attention until the man was standing right in front of me, flashing his police ID in my face.

As they forced me into their car, I prayed silently but fervently, "God help me!"

Immediately, I felt an unbelievable peace come over me.

It was like fiction unrolling, a story happening in my body. My mind and emotions were amazingly tranquil, almost on a different level from my actions. I was jammed into the back seat between two men, cramped, grubby from playing basketball, speeding down bumpy roads in the darkness.

I couldn't move. One guy was sitting against me to pin me in on the right, and the other held my left arm in a wrestling hold.

---

4 Alka was thirteen years old and had been playing basketball with Herb, who was coaching him that afternoon. Alka was a member of Herb and Linda's Christian fellowship group.

Everybody in Dagestan knew something about wrestling; they prided themselves on being some of the best wrestlers in the world.

I struggled to reach for the driver, to stop him or at least to upset the apple cart enough to get out, but the men jerked me back and kept restraining me—I was theirs! This meant big trouble for me, but I only felt an unearthly calm from God as I was pinned here, trapped between the two kidnappers.

The man on my left yanked my sock cap down over my eyes.

"Be still," he said in Russian.[5] "Be calm. It will only be a few months until you are freed."

I really should have been more alert. A week earlier, after playing basketball, I had been accosted by four cops and a KGB-type looking man on my way home. The location was only yards from the front entrance to our apartment complex. It was close to home, so I tried to ignore them. They were off to the right, standing around waiting around for me as I walked toward the door. They hailed me. I ignored them, but they called again. They wore dark police uniforms and searched me and my sports bag

"Do you have a pistol?" they asked.

I got mad and said, "Yeah."

It was all a ploy to see exactly what time I would be there and if I were truly harmless. Once in our apartment, I furiously complained about this encounter to Linda, not realizing that they had just "cased" me out.

We didn't drive far. It was only minutes until we came to a quick stop and scrambled out of the car. Peeking through the knitting of my sock cap, I could tell we had stopped beside a house. It was an old wooden residence, probably on the outskirts of town. The men hustled me into the house.

---

5 Many local languages and dialects exist in the North Caucasus region, including in the republics of Dagestan and Chechnya. Because of Russia's traditional dominance, in the region, the common language of communication among so many diverse cultures and peoples is Russian, the basics of which Herb and Linda learned in Moscow before moving to Dagestan.

There were several rooms, and no one else was inside. The place was pretty empty. The men took me into an ugly old room that was all wood. They ordered me to sit down on a bed. One of them approached me holding a roll of green tape, and he pulled off a long strip to bind my hands together. I sat passively while still feeling that amazing God-breathed peace.

A small wooden trap door blended in with the floor of the room. They opened the trap door, and two men lowered me down into a cellar. Then they closed the little door over me. It was pitch black. I lay on a mattress, calm and unafraid, listening to the sound of the men's footsteps fading away.

Not too long after—at most an hour or two—the men returned and hoisted me back up. They sat me down on the bed again, and the crew left, leaving one of them behind as a guard. I recognized this man as the same one who had put the wrestling hold on me in the car. He was tall, slender, clean-shaven—a nondescript Russian-looking guy. He paced back and forth noisily, scraping the wooden floor with his boots.

"How much money is in your house?" he asked me.

I had just gone to the bank earlier in the day and had accidentally exchanged too much money, so I knew exactly how much was at home.

"There's a thousand dollars there," I said, speaking to him in Russian, and naively tried to talk him into taking that money and letting me go. He wasn't convinced. I had no idea how much he and his comrades were going to be paid for kidnapping me.

"What's in your bag?"

"There's some money in there," I told him. "Inside is my day timer, and hidden inside that is a hundred dollar bill."

Most of the recent kidnappings in the Dagestani-Chechen region happened for money, and this guy was probably involved for the same reason. He seemed to have some financial worries, and I guessed this must have been a last measure for him. It didn't seem like he, personally, wanted to hurt me. In the car, he said that I would only be held for a few months at most.

"Oh, for a million dollars," he sighed, still pacing back and forth. "Or fifty thousand!"

The man's bizarre reasoning seemed ridiculous to me. He continued to pace, moaning about his personal troubles, while I sat on the bed, hands still bound and blindfolded.

"Oh, life is so difficult!" he exclaimed. "My life has so many problems!"

"Well, kidnapping me won't solve your problems," I retorted.

He paused, then asked about our missionary activities. He didn't seem to understand why Linda and I would choose to live and work in Dagestan, a place where we wouldn't make much money.

"For whose sake are you working here?" he asked.

"For God's sake!" I exclaimed.

I was surprised at my boldness, though my troubled captor didn't react.

"Don't you know that God loves you?" I asked him.

The man huffed, "Yeah? Does he?"

He sounded doubtful, too absorbed by his own problems to think about this possibility.

Just the two of us were in the room. I didn't try to run. After my experience in the car, my senses told me that an attempted escape would fail. There was no gun around, though he probably figured he didn't need one, knowing I was without a weapon.

Shortly after my conversation with this kidnapper, his accomplices came back into the room and told me to lie down on the bed. It was an old double bed with a blanket. I cooperated, lying down on the blanket, on my side. One of my abductors gave me an injection to make me sleep—he said it was morphine. A couple of the men stayed in the room while the others left, and I laid there silently with the sock cap over my eyes, unable to sleep.

"Are you going to sleep?" the man who gave me the shot asked.

"No."

I felt wide awake. It was a strange feeling to be lying down in some unknown place, wide awake, but not at all anxious or worried. I prayed constantly, as I had been doing since these abductors first hauled me into the car. It was hard to know what to think or do in this situation, so I stayed on the bed, quietly praying, waiting for time to pass.

The shot-giver didn't sleep, either. He would ask me every hour, "Are you going to sleep? Are you going to sleep?"

"No," I replied.

He chuckled. "*Ariol*," he called me—"an eagle." Apparently, this was a compliment.

The hours ticked by. Before daybreak, the other men returned, and we were soon again on the move, rolling somewhere in a car. They kept the cap over my eyes, and I felt disoriented. I had no idea where we were going, just waiting calmly in the back seat, listening to the sound of the engine and the tires crunching stones beneath us. There was little conversation.

Hour after hour we kept moving along. By the time the sun rose, and morning came, we were in the country—a long way from Makhachkala. Our car stopped, and my captors pulled me out. We set off walking through fields in the crisp morning air. One of them cut the tape off my wrists—they felt they could trust me enough—and removed the cap covering my eyes.

We soon walked up to another car sitting on the side of a dirt road. Two men were waiting in that car, both of whom looked like ethnic Dagestanis. They wore civilian clothes and Russian fur caps with ear flaps. I was transferred to their car before my original abductors departed back through the fields. The new men did not say anything to me, and I did not try to speak to them.

We rode along dirt roads for a while, then halted. All three of us got out of the car and walked a short distance until we came to a point overlooking a valley. We stood at the top of a steep, rocky slope where I could gaze at the landscape. I was instantly struck by its breathtaking beauty. My suspicion was that we were near the border of neighboring Chechnya.

The slope ran down several hundred yards, then leveling slightly to join a large valley. A long, long way down at the bottom of the valley was a deep winding ravine. It seemed like someone could easily get lost down there. The valley was rocky, brown, and gray; the only vegetation was some low green plants clinging to the slope. Snow lay in patches on the ground.

All around were vast mountains, gorgeous, stunning, and rugged. The peaks were half covered in snow, half in shadow. This location was starkly majestic, a beauty unique to the Caucasus region. It was very much a wilderness area. Nobody was around for miles—nobody to watch a man get beaten or killed. There was nothing to be seen except rocks, mountains, and snow.

I thought, "This would be a good place to die."

--

The first time I heard about Dagestan was when Linda and I still lived in Portugal. We had been living there for a number of years, working with TEAM, The Evangelical Alliance Mission. Our last year there, before we moved to Moscow, I read a book called *Operation Soviet Union* that detailed all the types of people in the U.S.S.R. It was not long after the Soviet Union collapsed in 1991, during the time when Russia was opening up and a lot of missions were going into various Russian satellite countries. The book mentioned Dagestan, its incredible ethnic diversity, and the need for Christians to come and interact face to face with the people.

We wanted to go someplace like that: an area not yet reached, a place with over thirty ethnic groups, mostly Muslim in their faith, and devoid of the Christian gospel. We believed the needs were great, yet practically no missionaries were serving as witnesses in the northern Caucasus region.

Linda and I knew there were many risks in serving as missionaries there. One of our Russian language teachers in Moscow was appalled that we had decided to go to Dagestan. He tried to talk us out of such a move. But it was like a dream come true for Linda and me in being able to access and witness—in the Russian language—to so many ethnic subcultures. We felt moved that God had created this small window in time, this brief opportunity to connect with all the different people, since the Dagestanis had learned to speak Russian during their seventy years of dominating Soviet rule.

In the spring of 1995, two other missionaries and I went on a survey trip to the region. The weather was cold when we arrived in Makhachkala.[6] The city itself was poor and rundown, but the people were very warm, interesting, and hospitable. We made an appointment to visit Sheikh Ismailov, the president of the Pedagogical University. While we were in his office, he asked us to join him at a faculty party that evening. For entertainment, everyone enjoyed vigorous guitar playing and singing. The men offered elaborate toasts over a seven-course meal. We felt very welcome and had a great time.

While in a vehicle with President Ismailov, who was driving us back to our hotel after dinner, he invited us to come and work with the students at the university. That night, the three of us sat in our room in an old, ex-Soviet hotel, praying and praising the Lord. At that time of prayer, we came to believe that the hand of God was leading us to become His Christian witnesses in Dagestan.

Back in Moscow, we met weekly and continued to pray about the matter. At the end of that summer, Linda and I moved to Makhachkala. Two other couples and a single gentleman had arrived before us, and our close friend Christine Smithson came later. Every day throughout our time in Dagestan, we all met to pray. We believed and we knew that God could do big Acts-type miracles in this unreached area.

---

6 The capital city of Dagestan nestled next to the Caspian sea, had a population of around 350,000 during the 1990s. The overall population in Dagestan during the same decade was an estimated 2,000,000.

Linda and I taught at the university, at a grade school, and also at a teacher training center for teachers who came from all over Dagestan. We made friends with our students and other teachers, and many of them came to visit our home, a comfortable apartment in a relatively safe section of Makhachkala. (There were really no fully safe areas!)

One Christmas, we had 35 people at home with us, and it was wonderful just to be with them. We constantly sought ways to serve our friends and other people in the city—whether students, orphans, prisoners, or bankers—to help them if they had needs and to extend to them God's love.

Some of the people we met expressed interest in spiritual matters. As we shared our Christian beliefs and faith, some of them spoke about difficulties in their personal circumstances, and they asked about the joy and peace they saw in our lives. By late 1995, we began having evangelistic meetings and Bible teachings in our colleague's apartment—the beginning of our church. These gatherings quickly matured into a richly meaningful fellowship of Dagestani believers.

One ministry I always had pursued over the years involved sports. Since my father was a basketball coach back in Arizona, I grew up loving sports.[7] In Makhachkala, I taught basketball and ping pong—any number of sports that offered the opportunity to work with interested boys and men wanting to learn more about success in athletics.

About a year after our arrival in Makhachkala, I went into a building at the university where I had heard there was a weight room. The door monitor of the building was a young man named Timur.[8] Students were commonly assigned to be door monitors,

---

7 Herbert Alton Gregg., (1918-2012), played varsity basketball at the University of Missouri, served in the Navy during World War II, and later worked for twenty-five seasons as the head basketball coach at Northern Arizona University. A gifted athlete, he also was the long-time golf coach at NIU.

8 Timur was in his late teens and became an active member of the Gregg's Christian

and he happened to be on duty that day. He showed me to the weightlifting room. Timur had never been at that post before, and he never had that assignment again. So our meeting was fortuitous, a real blessing for both of us.

Timur turned out to be a really pleasant, intelligent, and sensitive young man. He wanted to improve his English, so I started helping him. In turn, he helped me with Russian. We'd meet a couple times a week, sitting and talking, switching between languages. Some weeks passed before Timur and I began having spiritual conversations. He was an honest, shy, sweet, sincere person, and he steadily became more interested in the Christian faith.

He asked, "Do you have a meeting?"

I invited him to our Sunday morning, 10 a.m. gathering held in the library. Timur sent his younger brother Marat to scope out our fellowships. Marat was a bit more outgoing and courageous than Timur. He enjoyed the fellowship; he especially liked the praise music. Both of these young men started attending regularly. Soon, their whole family joined our worship meetings.

God had prepared them. Timur was really interested in the Bible—his ability to understand Scripture was impressive—and he eventually began preaching at our fellowships. Marat was a musician, leading our worship. Their father became an elder. He was an educated man who also had been in military service, and he was unusually upright. He was honest in his business dealings, very exceptional in a region dominated by Mafia-like criminal activity. He was a true nonconformist, persevering, with wonderful Christ-like qualities.

Over time, members of the fellowship started reaching out to others in need of God's love. Marat came to play basketball with me at the orphanage every Wednesday. He brought another fellow who became the first of fifteen people I baptized in Makhachkala.

---

fellowship group.

As others joined the fellowship, we organized the people into different Bible study groups; and they grew in their faith by leaps and bounds. The atmosphere was sweet, and we could see them gaining an understanding of God's glorious truths. They learned to take responsibility for leadership in our home gatherings and also in their other fellowships.

Everybody had a sense of our work having a special meaning for them. Nobody knew how Russia would act or what might happen in relation to the recent bloody conflict in nearby Chechnya,[9] but we felt like we were in the right place at the right time. It was incredibly fulfilling and satisfying to locate in an unreached area—something I had desired to do for decades—and to see people encounter the love and light of our Lord Jesus.

What a gratifying time of service we had, a great Christian adventure and experience in following the will of God. The Lord had greatly blessed us as we took each step carefully along the way.

--

Somehow, four years of greatly blessed mission activity had unexpectedly brought me here, literally to this empty, beautiful valley somewhere in the middle of the Caucasus Mountains. My two new abductors indicated that I should follow them down the slope. It was a steep decline, around 45 degrees. We scampered down the hill until we came to a shepherd's cabin.

The cabin sat on a small flat field in the midst of the slope. It was all wood, an old, dilapidated shack. The door to the cabin was chained up and padlocked. One of the men had to work on the lock and chain to get the door open. Inside was a single room, about four yards square. It had an old bed covered with a sheepskin blanket and a plain wooden table and chairs. A gray stone chimney took up much of one wall.

---

9 The First Chechen War (1994-1996) involved Russian forces fighting against Chechen rebels, the latter numbers determined to gain complete political independence from the Soviet Federation.

I looked around the room, not knowing what would happen next, and prayed that I would not have to wait in this gloomy space for many hours.

It was midday on November 12 when we arrived there. We had hours to kill before nightfall, so the men allowed me to walk around outside. I showed myself to be friendly and docile, and they could tell I was not going to try to escape.

They treated me decently. They did not bind my hands or require me to wear the sock cap over my eyes. Not to be too identifiable, they just averted their faces from me or turned slightly when I looked their way.

My two new captors sat together by the shack, talking in low voices, while I walked in an oval circuit in the field nearby. Since I was wearing my tennis shoes, I stepped over the patches of snow. I stayed on the bare ground, walking for what seemed like hours while praying and feeling this unbelievable internal peace that could only have come from my heavenly Father.

When darkness came, we retreated into the cabin. One of the captors got a fire going in the fireplace. It was the only light inside, casting flickering shadows across the wooden floor and walls.

The men gave me a little food to eat, mutton and water. They sat around the table, speaking softly to each other. They said nothing to me and mostly tried to avoid eye contact with me. I was really tired, having gone all this time without sleep, so I laid down on the bed and covered myself with the old sheepskin blanket. This time I had no trouble falling asleep.

My captors apparently stayed awake all night. They were still and silent, one of them simply sitting near the fireplace, staring into the fire, waiting to complete my next transfer the next morning to my Chechen kidnappers.

Herb and Linda in Makhachkala, Dagestan, circa 1997.

II

NIGHTMARE NEWS

LINDA

November 11, Makhachkala

Five-thirty and dinner was about ready.

"Where is he?" I wondered to myself, a little annoyed. I stood over the mashed potatoes, stirring slowly and adding milk to keep them from drying out, waiting for Herb to arrive.

Exasperated, I sighed and checked the clock again. It was already moving toward six. I sat down in the kitchen and asked myself if I should be worried.

Suddenly, there was a loud beating at the front door. Alarmed, I rushed over and opened it. Already dark, the concrete stairwell beyond our door was dim and cold. Light from our apartment shone past me and lit up two figures standing outside: Christine and Marat.

In chorus, they asked, "Is Herb here?"

"No, isn't he with you?"

Christine and Marat both helped Herb teach basketball at the orphanage every Wednesday afternoon. They glanced at each other and then stood mutely; they were obviously extremely disturbed that Herb wasn't home. They looked frightened. Their faces were white and strained, and they were panting for air. They must have run up the stairs, Herb and I lived on the third floor of our apartment building. I realized that something bad had happened just by looking at them.

"What's wrong?" I asked.

They didn't seem able to speak. I stared at Christine. In the years we had been working together in Dagestan, I had never seen her look so worried. Her pretty face was pale and seemed even whiter surrounded by her long dark hair and black jacket.

Finally, Marat spoke up. "Herb and Alka were walking down the street from the orphanage and . . . and there was an accident."

"An accident?" I imagined them being hit by a car.

"Have Herb and Alka been run over?"

"No," Marat said. He hesitated.

Marat was in his late teens. Herb and I had spent a lot of time getting to know and love him and his family over the last couple of years. I waited for Marat to continue, though he didn't.

There was another long, strained pause, and I anxiously looked back and forth at the two of them before Christine finally blurted out, "Some men pulled Herb into a car. Alka ran back to the orphanage to tell us what happened. We rushed over here to see if he was wrong, or if Herb had been able to escape."

My heart stopped for a moment. Shocked and appalled, it was hard for me to think clearly. Herb's been abducted. Why? What does that mean? We all stood on the doorstep, staring at each other, trying to comprehend that Herb was being whisked away somewhere. Kidnapped? What a horrible situation.

The air was icy.

I managed to squeak out, "Come inside."

Christine and Marat followed me into the warmth of the apartment. Each of them stopped to give me a hug as they entered, and I closed the door behind them.

"What should we do?" Even to me, my voice sounded distant.

We stood in the hall entryway, near the phone. Christine and Marat started offering possibilities: Whom should we call? The police? Did we know anyone with the police?

My mind was buzzing, but my body could hardly function. While they debated whom to call, I just stood there, weakly nodding at various suggestions.

Somebody decided we should call the OVIR office—the government office that issued our visas. In a way, they were responsible for us, and we had spent a lot of time down there turning in papers and giving interviews, so the office workers knew who we were.

This conversation kept us busy for a minute. I wanted to do something quickly, not stand around in confusion while Herb was being kidnapped.

Christine took charge and started dialing.

She held the phone up to her ear and looked my way. I knew she was concerned about me. Christine was always sensitive and attentive to anyone in need, and I loved her like a daughter. She had a habit of appearing at anyone's side whenever they needed her support.

The lady who answered at the government office expressed mortification when Christine told her the news about Herb.

"Are you sure?" she asked.

"Yes," Christine affirmed. "It happened not far from the orphanage. A young boy who was with him witnessed the abduction."

The lady said how terribly sorry she was, and how surprised. There had been some other foreigners kidnapped in the area over the past few years, but they had been temporary workers who had no connections or protection and were therefore vulnerable. We had been living there for nearly four years.

Christine thanked the lady and hung up the phone, saying, "She said she would send the police over right away."

I was relieved things were *finally* in motion. Maybe the police could catch the kidnappers before they got too far away. We walked from the hallway into the living room to wait for the police to arrive.

I was still in shock. I felt the beginning of panic; my heart was beating a hundred miles an hour. We were really helpless to stop what was happening—to thwart the abductors who had taken Herb.

"Let's sit down and pray," I suggested.

I prayed first, asking God to protect Herb, to help him get away or to stop the kidnappers. Somewhere in the back of my mind, I was desperately hoping that this heartbreaking matter would all end quickly, that Herb would walk through the door, and we wouldn't have to worry anymore. Surely his abduction was a mistake!

As soon as I finished praying, a scene flashed through my mind from our youth meeting the previous Saturday. Christine and Marat continued to pray, though I was no longer listening to them.

Saturday the youth finished with their Bible study early; we had a little extra time, so we did something we'd never done before. We went around the group and each person told of one way they had seen the Lord working in somebody else's life. When it got to my turn, I picked Herb. For some reason, I had the desire to tell him that he was the most faithful person to the Lord I had ever known—in big matters and in small things—and how much I loved him.

Now, suddenly, I understood why God had *let* me say that at the time, knowing how hard it would be for me to cope with Herb's being kidnapped, maybe to never see him again, not having told him how I much I loved him.

"God knew on Saturday that this was going to happen today, on Wednesday," I recognized.

God was indeed sovereign. He gave me this gift, knowing that Herb was going to be kidnapped. He assured me that I wasn't alone, that He was with both Herb and me. I felt reassured that we were not serving Him in the wrong location at the wrong time. God was omnipotent, He was still in control; we were exactly where we should be, and everything would be okay. God would provide complete protection. My racing heart slowed, and I could feel myself calm down. I thought, "It's going to be okay."

The realization that God had allowed me to tell Herb of my love for him five days before he was kidnapped, gave me a deep rooted belief that I needed to keep my eyes on Him and not on the circumstances. It also fixed my hope on God and His powers of good, not on people through the stressful days to come.

We asked so much as we prayed. I appreciated that my hope was well placed in His hands. Remembering His goodness gave me great peace in my heart.

After we prayed, I decided to call our TEAM leader in Moscow, Phil Cantrell, to tell him what happened. When I told him, he didn't believe it?[10]

"Herb has been kidnapped," I said.

"No. No, this can't be right. . . . It must be a mistake."

"Yes, he was returning home from the orphanage; they grabbed him off the street, he's gone, and he's not coming home."

"Well, maybe we should wait a few hours before calling the home office, just in case it is a mistake."

I understood what he was hoping.

"It's not a mistake," I assured Phil, "but if you want to wait, that's okay. We'll call you back later. The police are on their way over now."

I hung up the phone and checked the time. Where were the police?

Christine and Marat were sitting in the living room quietly talking. I wanted to speak with my daughter Amy in the U.S., so I dialed the phone again. It rang and rang before the answering machine picked up, indicating that nobody was home.[11] I left a message telling her I had something important to talk with her

---

10 Up to this point in time, no U. S. citizen living in Dagestan or Chechnya had been abducted. However, other Christian missionaries had been, and ransom payments had secured their freedom to return to their homes. Phil Cantrell would have known that kidnappings were commonplace but to learn that one of his close associates had been abducted with no idea of where Herb was had to be shocking.

11 Amy Gregg Glover, twenty-five-years-old, was then living in Phoenix, Arizona, with her husband Steve and their baby son Caleb. Amy was active in her local church while taking special care of Caleb, who was born with a fatal disease.

about, so she needed to call me as soon as possible. In a way, I was relieved to get the machine; I didn't want to tell her the news—but I was also frustrated. I felt like I needed a connection with her, with my family back home in the U. S.

I sat back down in the living room to wait. Christine and Marat told me more about the events at the orphanage. The physical education teacher had sprained her ankle, so they stayed to put ice on it and to have some tea. Meanwhile, Herb left with Alka, but he ran back later and told them about the men forcing Herb into the car. Christine and Marat didn't have many more details, since they took off immediately for our apartment.

More time began to pass, and still no police arrived. I shot a look of distress toward the front door. If this were a fire, I mused, the whole building would be burned to the ground by now! There wasn't anything we could do but sit around and wait. We had to trust the government lady to call the police and then trust the police to do what they could to help rescue Herb.

I sighed and leaned back into the chair, glad that my hope was in the Lord and not in the Makhachkala police.

--

Finally, there was a loud knocking at the door. Quickly I opened the door. Four police officers barged into the apartment and spread out around the room. They wore dark uniforms and hats and stood up straight, looking very official. The captain wanted to know who I was. I stated my name and that this was our apartment. He pointed to Christine and Marat and tersely asked who they were, sounding a bit irritated that extra people might be involved with his investigation. I identified them and stated how they would know some things that I didn't.

The captain then told me that they were the police responsible for the section of Makhachkala where Herb had been abducted. He asked if I knew what had happened. I gestured toward Christine and Marat, and they briefly related Alka's story to the captain.

Standing to the side, I noticed that the police officers at first appeared very proper and capable, acting like they knew exactly what they were doing. But watching intently and listening to them, I started to wonder if they had any idea of what was going on. The captain didn't ask Christine and Marat any pertinent questions about Herb. In fact, he didn't seem to care much about the kidnapping. They were all gazing around the apartment.

One of the officers took out some paper and started to make a rough sketch of our apartment plan. The captain came over to me and began asking questions about each room. We started a slow tour around our apartment.

The captain looked into our bedroom.

"This is where you sleep?" he asked.

"Yes," I replied. I was confused about the purpose of these questions.

"You and your husband?"

"Yes."

We moved on to the guest room. In my mind, I had a picture of Herb's captors fleeing with him from the city while the police were drawing up the floor plans of our apartment.

"Is this a guest room?"

"Yes."

"Who stays here?"

"Nobody."

We continued to the living room.

I wondered, "Is this some kind of a joke?"

"This is a nice big living room," the captain said pleasantly. "Do you have many people in?"

"Yes, we have a lot of friends. We teach at the university."

"This must be the dining room over here. Oh, nice dining room."

We moved along to the kitchen, even to the bathroom. One officer kept sketching the whole time, everything in detail. I wondered what this had to do with anything but decided to just answer their questions. They were so formal, I didn't dare laugh, but I thought again how glad I was that my hope was not in these people but in the Lord.

The police stayed for about twenty minutes, finished the drawing and then left, saying they would be back in a few minutes. I closed the door behind them and sat back down in the living room with Christine and Marat.

Christine looked at me in amazement and asked, "What in the world was that all about?"

I shook my head.

--

Not five minutes later, there was knocking at the door again.

"That was quick," I thought. "A 'few minutes' was right!"

Impressed with their efficiency, I got up and opened the door. Standing outside in the chilly stairwell was an entirely different group of police officers, wearing similar dark uniforms and acting as official as the first group. When they came into the apartment, their captain told me that they were the police responsible for the area of Makhachkala where our apartment was located. The police officers spread around the room, and the captain asked us all the same questions.

One of the officers pulled out some paper and started making a sketch of the apartment. The captain pointed to our bedroom.

We started the exact same route around the house, discussing everything as before. Was this what they learned in police school?

Halfway through the inspection, about the time we reached the dining room, there was again loud knocking on the front door. I was curious. The captain accompanied me, and I opened the door to find the first group of police officers. The captain of this group smiled at me and walked right in, but his smile froze as soon as he saw the second group standing in our apartment, drawing their own set of impromptu blueprints.

The second captain angrily said something to the first captain. The first captain replied brusquely, and a heated argument started about who was officially in charge. I couldn't understand everything they said, but the two police groups stood facing each other, firing verbal shots back and forth in Russian across my entry hall for about five minutes. In the end, the first group—those from the zone where Herb had been abducted—stormed out of the apartment. We never saw them, or their drawing, again.

The second captain continued on with his questioning, but I stopped him and asked, "Is anybody looking for the car or the men who abducted Herb?"

"Oh, yeah," he said. "I'll make a call."

He immediately dialed a number and asked whether check points were set up on all roads leading out of Makhachkala, By this point in time, I was sure the captors could have been well on their way to Chechnya, or to wherever they were taking Herb.

The captain didn't seem surprised by my question, so I hoped that check points were already in place. He was so much more official than any of the other police officers that he probably felt he should be doing something to make me feel better.

The captain then told me that he was a personal friend of the president of the university, Sheikh Ismailov, where we taught English. "Let me give him a call," he offered.

Dagestan has a dominant Islamic culture, even though a part of Russia. In their culture, if a guest were hurt, the host would be obligated to avenge that hurt, even to their own death. I understood that as guests of the university, they were culturally the most responsible for us. I knew it was possible the Lord could now use such an influential person as the president, and I was thankful we had a very positive relationship with him.

I listened to the captain exchange greetings with the president; then he told about Herb. The president asked the captain to express to me how sorry he was and that he would do everything he could to help get Herb released.

During the phone call, there was another knock at the door. It was Timur, Marat's brother. Timur was a few years older than Marat; both young men had a slender build and short blonde hair. Both were bright and capable--valuable leaders in our church.

Herb first met Timur at the university about a year after we arrived in Dagestan. We explained to him all that had happened so far.

--

Soon after the police captain finished his conversation with the university president, the phone rang—another call for him. He spoke for a moment, then lowered the phone and looked over at me.

"Did Herb have a sports bag with him?" he asked.

"He had one when he left the house," I said, describing the bag to him. "I don't know if he had it when he left the orphanage."

Marat said Herb had left the orphanage with it.

The captain talked awhile longer with the person on the phone and then hung up.

"We need to take you down to the police station," he said, specifying me, Christine, and Marat. "No sports bag has been found, so we will first go to the place where your husband was taken to see if the bag is still there."

I put on my coat and followed the captain and another police officer out the front door. It was about nine o'clock now, very dark, and a cold, bitter November night. Christine and Marat came along with me; Timur stayed at the apartment in case anybody called. We all piled into the police car and set off to the abduction site. My heart was in my throat just thinking about seeing the abduction location.

We wound our way through town and turned onto a long, straight, narrow road. It was really dark. There was no light except for the car's headlights, which shone faintly down the road, revealing a row of solid metal fences on either side. The fences stood tall next to the car, but slowly disappeared from sight as they stretched out in front of us, as we followed the road into the black night.

The neighborhood was old, featuring small houses and barbed wire. Privacy and security were priorities here, and people in the houses apparently didn't want anyone to see in or see out. Nobody would have noticed Herb's being forced into a car, though an entire family might have been only steps away.

There didn't seem to be any place nearby where the bag could be hidden. The police officer pulled out a flashlight and clicked it on. He and the captain got out of the car and started looking around the road. I sat and watched the two obscure figures move their zigzagging beam of light around the base of the fences.

"So this is where Herb was abducted," I thought.

I couldn't believe they had brought me to the scene of the crime. It seemed weird to be right where Herb had been grabbed off the road, maybe from the very spot where our car had stopped. I sat right in the middle of the back seat, wondering where Herb had been taken next, and where he was now in the pitch black darkness beyond the small puddle of light created by our car.

I wondered if they would find the bag. Were they looking for Herb as much as they were looking for that sports bag?

After a few minutes, the captain and police officer returned to the car. They had found nothing. We drove off down the street toward the orphanage but slowed to a crawl when we approached a vacant lot near the orphanage. The captain said they were looking for an abandoned police car. We all strained to see out the windows, though there was no police vehicle anywhere to be seen. We sped up and drove past the orphanage, on toward the police station.

The station was a small, single-story gray concrete building. It was plain and unlit from the outside. There was nothing attractive about this police headquarters.

As we got out of the car, my legs didn't want to move, I was very nervous and cold. Under these conditions my multiple sclerosis made me stiff as a board. Christine held on to me and encouragingly helped me make my way into the station.

I felt apprehensive coming here. Why did they want us to be at this location? We weren't the ones who had kidnapped anybody.

Once inside, I would never have guessed we were standing in a police station. The interior was so bare, so stark and dimly lit. The walls were colorless, undecorated except for a small calendar. The air was smoky.

Only a few uniformed officers were inside the station, and there was no activity despite someone's having been kidnapped. Those who were there smiled politely at me and tried to act busy.

We followed the captain down a hallway to the right, and he ushered us into a boxy little room that must have been an office. In the middle was a desk with a chair on either side; a few more chairs were lined up along the edge of the room. On one side of the desk was a serious-looking police officer holding a pen over a stack of paper. On the other side of the desk was young Alka.

When we entered the room and sat down, the police officer was in the process of asking Alka a series of questions.

"What color was the man's coat?" The policeman's attitude was somewhat hostile. Did they think Alka was involved in the kidnapping?

Alka sat with his hands on his lap, calm and cool.

"Black," he said.

The police officer scribbled something down on the paper. He wrote and wrote and wrote. I wondered if it really took him that long to write "black."

"Did he say anything?"

"Yes."

"What?"

"He said that they were police and that Herb should come with them."

The police officer wrote and wrote and wrote.

"What did Mr. Gregg say?"

"He didn't pay any attention. He just kept walking, and I followed him."

Alka was a short, sturdy boy with dark eyes and dark hair in a crew cut that lay forward onto his forehead. I liked Alka—he was a polite, respectful lad. He liked Herb a lot, and Herb enjoyed spending time with him.

Alka glanced over at me while the police officer kept writing intensely. He kept responding as the police officer asked his questions; and Alka told him everything he knew. Once they finished, the police officer started the series of questions all over again.

"What time did you leave the orphanage?"

"A few minutes after 5 o'clock, it was almost dark."

"Did Mr. Gregg have anything with him?"

"He had his sports bag."

"What was in the bag?"

"I don't know."

"What happened on the road?"

"A car drove up slowly alongside us. We ignored it."

"What kind of car was it?"

"It was a big white car."

The police officer continued to write at length after asking each question.

"Then what happened?"

"The car drove a little ahead of us and stopped. Two large men got out."

"What were they wearing?"

"Regular clothes—pants and coats. Not uniforms."

I listened carefully. It was interesting and good for me to hear Alka's interrogation, because I was hearing details regarding what happened to Herb. I was so grateful Alka was with Herb at the time—if he hadn't been there, we wouldn't have known anything.

Alka and Herb did not want to wait around the orphanage after practice, so Herb offered to accompany Alka home. They were walking down the road when the men jumped out, claiming to be police officers. Herb tried to ignore them, but one of the men stood right in front of him, holding up a badge. The moment Herb stopped the second man came up from behind and grabbed him around the neck.

It was all so fast, Alka said. Herb started flailing, shaking, and fighting the men as they tried to drag him into the car. Alka stated that he ran up to the man holding Herb and jumped on his back, but the man threw him off, telling him to get lost. Alka scrambled to his feet and backed up against the large metal fence, watching to get as much information as possible.

For a few minutes, the two men fought with Herb, trying to get him into the car. One of the attackers was tall, with dark hair. Tall was not common in Dagestan—many Dagestanis were short and strong. Looking past the struggling figures, Alka noticed two other men sitting in the front seat. He could not describe them. There was some sort of light near them, perhaps coming from a cell phone, he thought.

Herb was all over the place fighting. Finally, Alka said, the first man managed to get a hold of Herb's feet and pull them up. Then the two men shoved Herb into the back seat, got in beside him and shut the doors.

Once the men were in the car, Alka darted out to see what kind of vehicle it was and to get the license plate number. The car was a Zhiguli.[12] It had no plates. The vehicle started off down the road, then suddenly stopped and lurched before speeding away. Alka said that he feared Herb was fighting to get out and worried that they might have hurt him more as a result. When the car disappeared

12 This car was a Russian made automobile of four-door design. At this point in time, this boxy looking car sold under the brand name Lada. Not a large vehicle, it must have been very crowded with five people crammed into it.

around a corner, Alka turned and ran back toward the orphanage to tell Christine and Marat.

Not far from the orphanage, in a vacant lot, Alka noticed a police car. He ran over to get help. The car doors were open, but nobody was in it. He looked around but didn't see anyone there, so he ran on to the orphanage.

The police officer wrote endless pages of notes while Alka was speaking. I wondered what on earth he could be writing. When they finished questioning Alka the final time, the police officer handed the stack of papers over to him for his signature. One of the officers then took Alka and escorted him out of the room.

--

They next questioned me. I sat down in the chair by the desk and looked up at the police officer. His pen was already hovering over the paper. The officers were all polite, but they hadn't said much to me so far. I thought perhaps they were unsure of how much Russian I spoke, being a foreigner. Actually, my Russian wasn't that great but passable.

"What was your husband wearing when he left the orphanage?"

"I don't know."

"What was he wearing when he left home?"

I paused to think. "His leather coat, a flannel shirt, and some slacks," I said. Herb usually changed into jeans before playing basketball.

They asked about his shoes. I told them he had been wearing his good street shoes when he left and that he had a pair of tennis shoes with him for the basketball lesson.

"What did he have in his sports bag?"

"I am not sure," I said, "but I think he had his tennis shoes and an extra pair of socks." The police officer wrote madly. I was amused that he wrote so much and said so little.

"Did he have money in the bag?"

"Not much, if any."

"Did he have a weapon in the bag?"

"No."

He asked me a few mundane questions about our time in Dagestan: how long we had been here, what we were doing, what time Herb usually came home at night.

He also asked about Alka. They were suspicious of him. They thought that perhaps he helped set a trap, as he had been staying with relatives up in the mountains and had just recently returned home. I told them who Alka was and that I doubted he was involved. Herb had been so good to him, and he liked Herb so much. Since Alka had been out of town, Herb invited him to play basketball this afternoon to spend time together. I said I just couldn't imagine him wanting to hurt Herb. The police officer offered no reaction.

Despite my brief answers, the police officer wrote five pages during my interview. He slid the pages across the desk for me to sign. I glanced briefly at them, wondering what he had written. It really wasn't expected that I would read them, so I sighed, signed the bottom and passed them back. Formalities were important in Dagestan.

Then Marat was summoned. The police officer asked him several similar questions about what Herb was wearing and what he had with him when he left the orphanage. Marat knew more than I did. He said Herb left in the clothes that he wore after playing basketball for two hours: olive colored jeans, a sweaty t-shirt, and his green plaid flannel shirt. He was wearing his black leather jacket, his black sock cap, and tennis shoes. His good shoes were in the bag, and Herb had said he was going home to take a shower and change clothes.

Marat told the officer about the injured P.E. teacher and how he and Christine stayed to ice her ankle and drink hot tea. Herb did not want to drink hot tea after two hours of basketball. He said he was quite hungry and just wanted to get home and eat dinner. When Alka reappeared at the building, Marat hoped he was wrong about the kidnapping. He and Christine rushed outside and looked for a taxi to take them to our apartment.

Marat signed his stack of papers, and Christine took his place in the interrogation chair when a police officer approached and asked me to come out into another room. This officer was not wearing a uniform, and he didn't look like a Dagestani. I stood up stiffly and followed him outside.

The man introduced himself as a government officer from next door country Chechnya where they were having numerous problems with kidnappings. His specialty, he informed me, was working with kidnapping crimes. The government sent him to Dagestan to investigate reported abductions; he came to the station after hearing about Herb and had only just arrived in Makhachkala.

I quickly realized—from this man's demeanor, experience, and the relevance of the questions asked—that he was truly competent in his job. He was very pleasant, asking me about Herb and what we were doing in Dagestan and especially about the relationships we had with people in the area.

"Do you know anyone who would want to hurt Herb or see this happen to him?" he asked. The old vendetta system was strong in Dagestan, and revenge of this magnitude was common. I thought for a moment but couldn't think of anyone who would want to hurt Herb in some way.

The officer asked more questions about our life and the people we encountered from day to day. He asked about suspicious vendors, store clerks, coworkers, neighbors—people who might hold something against us. Fortunately, I did not know anyone who might be involved. On the contrary, Herb and I had many, many fine friends in the city.

The government officer and I spoke for about fifteen minutes.

"If you think of anyone who might be involved, please let me know," he requested.

"I will."

"Do not worry," he said. His manner was comforting. "I assure you we will be doing our best to find your husband."

"Thank you," I said and shook his hand.

I returned to the small office to wait while Christine finished her statement, verifying what Marat said happened at the orphanage. She signed another stack of papers from the police officer.

We rose from our chairs and walked toward the exit. I stopped in front of the head police officer and shook his hand, smiling my gratitude, but knowing that their efforts alone could not immediately rescue Herb. Right then Psalm 44:6-7 filled my mind: *For I will not trust in my bow, nor shall my sword save me. But You have saved us from our enemies, and have put to shame those who hated us.*

"I greatly appreciate everything you are doing to help," I told him, "but you need to know that really, my hope is in the Lord."

"Then together with the Lord, we will get the job done," he replied, surprising me. He gripped my hand tightly.

--

The time was almost midnight when we walked out into the bitter night air. It was so dark—pitch black all around. Behind us, dim light from inside the police station barely escaped through the windows. Straight ahead, at the end of the street, a small white police car sat in the road, its faint light revealing a police officer sitting at the wheel, ready to drive us home.

Suddenly I felt bone tired. My stiff, frozen body could hardly move. I looked up into the sky, to observe the bright, beautiful stars.

"God—help," I implored.

Christine and Marat walked on either side of me. I was moving like a tin soldier, but becoming more able to walk with every step. At the police car, I wondered if I would be able to make my legs bend enough to get in. Somehow, Christine and Marat helped me sit as we crammed into the car for the ride back to our apartment. The police officers who drove saw us to the door of our apartment before leaving, saying they would be back in the morning.

Timur met us at the door. My daughter had called several times while we were gone, he said. Timur spoke English very well, and he knew all about Amy and her family, but when she called, he did not have the heart to tell her what happened to Herb. He only said there was a problem and that she needed to call me back.

I decided to call Amy right away. Christine offered me a supportive nod, and then she took Timur and Marat away to make up beds in the guest room and living room. None of them had any intention of leaving me alone that night.

I walked slowly to the phone. Oh, how I dreaded this phone call! Everything that occurred was like a bad dream until now, but I knew telling Amy would make all reality true.

Amy answered the phone sounding more upset than I was. She knew something terrible had happened.

"Mom, what's the matter?"

"Amy," I stuttered, "Daddy's been kidnapped." "Amy," I stuttered again, "Daddy's been kidnapped." She gasped, "Oh, no!"

She started crying, and I started crying listening to her. This was the first time I let my tears flow. It was such a wrenching feeling to have to tell our daughter.

Amy couldn't believe it. I tried to encourage her, to explain that everything would be okay. I told her about our time of prayer and how God had given me peace and the knowledge that He was in control.

"We just need to pray and trust the Lord," I said.

She wanted some details, so I described the police station and Alka's story. I asked her to call our son Jason at college and to call our church and have them start praying.[13]

"Mom, is there anything you need?"

"Get everyone praying," I said. "That is all I need."

We said our goodbyes, and I promised to keep in touch.

I was heading off to get ready for bed, dragging my worn out body

13 Jason Gregg was nineteen years old in 1998 and taking college classes in the Phoenix area. He was in regular contact with his older sister Amy. In time he became an active missionary himself, taking on assignments in Taiwan and other locations.

across the living room, when the phone rang. It was our supervisor, Phil Cantrell, calling from Moscow.

"Linda," he said, "I called the home office. They've got things going on their end. They told everyone to start praying, and they're figuring out what to do. Don't worry about those details."

It was heartening to know that I had so many people standing alongside me in prayer, and others who were willing to work for Herb's release.

"But Linda . . ." he paused. "This is very important: you and Christine need to get out of Dagestan within twenty-four hours."

"What?"

"You have to leave, Linda," he said. He was insistent. "The kidnappers will try to contact you. You and Christine could be in danger."

I thought about the risks if we were to stay, and I recognized his fears. I thought about our friends and our thriving church. Twenty-four hours. There was too much to do in so short a time. I knew that I would never be able to come back, or at least not for a very long, very long time. I just couldn't say goodbye so fast.

"I don't think there's any way we can leave that soon," I responded, speaking as firmly as I could, being that exhausted.

Christine overheard our conversation and walked toward me to see what was wrong.

"I'm sorry, Linda, but your safety is in question." As a TEAM leader, his greatest concern was for our health and security.

"Well . . . okay," I relented. "We'll work out something. Christine and I will talk and call you back in the morning."

I hung up the phone.

"What's going on?" Christine asked.

I related everything about the twenty-four hour deadline. I explained my own thoughts as well. I knew in my heart that I would not be coming back for a long while, if ever again. I needed to see some of the people we loved. I needed closure. And I couldn't stand the idea of leaving so many friends—and Herb—behind in Dagestan.

Christine agreed with me. "It's too soon," she said. "We'll call him in the morning and ask for a few more days."

We had reached the end of a very long and difficult day. So much had happened. I stood in our bedroom, numb from exhaustion, trying not to think about everything that needed to be done in the coming days or weeks—however long Herb would be forcibly held by his captors.

I climbed into the bed, certain I would fall right asleep, but as I laid down in the dark without Herb there, the tears again began to flow. I put my hand over on his side and patted the bed, telling him everything would be okay. Somehow, I just felt closer to Herb, lying there, patting the place where he wasn't.

III

ONTO THE CHECHEN OUTPOST

Herb

November into December,

Initial Days of Incarceration

Before dawn on Friday, the 13th, of all days, we were up and out of the shepherd's cabin. We scrambled back up the steep slope toward the road. As I was climbing, I slipped, put my hand down and got stuck by a low green plant that dotted the ground. It was the only plant life around, and it was covered in stickers.

We reached the top of the slope and came to the spot in the road where we had been the day before. A jeep-like transport vehicle was waiting for us. It was large, some kind of military truck, with two rows of seating up front and two benches along the sides in its covered back.

A driver sat behind the wheel, and three others stood near the jeep's open back door. The men were wearing military khakis and boots. Their faces were not covered, but I didn't have much time to look at them.

I was quickly transferred to this new group, and now the rough stuff started. These were my Chechen captors: Mostly jihadis.[14]

One of the men kicked me into the back of the jeep. He pulled my sock cap down over my eyes and started slapping and hitting me—not hard, he was playing some kind of intimidation game. The rest of my new captors all piled in, and we were off. I sat on the bench running along the right side. The man hitting me sat on the opposite bench, and the other two squatted into seats in front of me.

Instantly, talking in Russian, they plied me with all manner of questions. If I gave an answer they didn't like, they would whack me.

They started asking a number of questions about who I was and my family.

"What's your name?"

"Where are you from in the States?"

"How old are you?"

"Do you have a wife? Any kids?"

They asked if I had been in the Army. I said yes, knowing what they meant—there was no point in explaining the difference between the Marines and the Army. In their minds, a person who had been in the armed forces was more likely to be a resister or a spy.

I answered all of their questions. My main thought was to cooperate. From the beginning, I sensed that it was important for me to cooperate with them and not to fight.

"Are you Jewish?" they asked.

"No," I replied, a little surprised at their question.

"Is your wife?"

"No."

"Your parents?"

They started asking about my and Linda's lineage, wanting to

---

14 Herb used the word "jihadi" throughout his recollections to describe those he was sure were Muslim extremists His captors were most likely fundamentalist Wahhabi sect believers. Generally, moderate Muslims would not have exhibited such hatred toward Jews, but Wahhabi Muslims often expressed strong anti-Semitic sentiments.

know if we had any Jewish relatives. I did not mention Linda's Jewish grandfather.

They also asked about our friends and acquaintances; they were really checking me out on how many Jews I knew. They couldn't believe that I knew only one man who was Jewish–they thought all Americans had a great many Jewish friends.

The man who was sitting across from me reached over and deftly removed my wedding ring and watch. I felt really bad about losing the ring.

"What are you doing in Dagestan?"

"I'm with a humanitarian organization," I explained. "We teach, we work at the orphanage and different places. We try to help the people of Makhachkala in every way we can: educationally, socially, spiritually . . ."

"Spiritually? What do you do spiritually?"

I described how we were starting a fellowship of Christian believers, a church. I said that we were trying to help people in all ways and that included spiritual aspects.

The men were very antagonistic. They treated me like an invader. The captor across from me said that the spiritual matter was the worst thing I was doing in Dagestan.

"Why are you doing this?" he demanded.

I quoted Revelation 1:5, saying, "*He loves us, and the blood of Jesus Christ separates us from all sin.*"

This Scripture made him furious. He gave me several slugs around the head and shoulders.

"What do you mean, separates us from all sin?!" he asked, rather violently.

They recognized that I was a Christian. "*Yégesh*," the man called me. It was a hate term for Christians. My thought was that maybe I should be more discreet after this episode, but even so, it did not make me feel desperate. The man across from me, the one who hit me, called himself Hassan. He was especially hostile.

The fellow who sat in front of me asked, "What do you know about Islam?" He asked his questions more calmly than Hassan.

"Not too much," I replied. I didn't know a whole lot about Islam, and I thought it would be better for them to believe that I was acting out of ignorance. I wasn't a Muslim, they would conclude, because I didn't know how good their religion was. Later I discovered that, in fact, they did think I was just ignorant of the goodness of the Islamic faith.

As we rode along, the driver jokingly asked if I wanted a hamburger. I chuckled, and Hassan punched me again. The jihadis wanted me to feel dependent on them out of fear and respect, and they did not want me in a cheerful mood.

They forced me to lie down on my side so I couldn't see, even though I was still wearing the sock cap. After a while, my neck hurt, and they allowed me to lie prone on my back. They gave me nuts to eat and a soft drink.

After what seemed like a long ride, we arrived at the "outpost." This building was a converted Soviet-built school with a long middle section and perpendicular wings on each side. I didn't see it from the outside, but inside it was plain, mostly concrete. There were school rooms, cement stairs, hallways—all big and empty, with very high ceilings. The building was fairly dim, with hanging bulbs for lighting. There were three floors, and the jihadis quickly placed me in a dark little room on the second floor.

Hassan and the other man—I called him "Cap" for "Captor"—had me empty my pockets and give them the contents. There wasn't much: a pocket knife and some coins. They put these items in a plastic bag and probably stored them with bags belonging to other kidnap victims.

They took my belt and tennis shoes as well. I still had my leather coat and my sweat socks on, and I was wearing my street socks underneath those, for warmth. My sports bag was gone; my initial captors back in Makhachkala had taken it.

Cap and Hassan explained to me that I had to be on all fours with my face in the corner and with my sock cap over my eyes whenever anyone entered my room. They didn't want me to see their faces.

"You won't get out of here without a ransom payment," Cap snarled at me before leaving the room, shutting and locking the door.

When they were gone, I pulled off my sock cap and looked around. The room was small—so very small—and dark. It was a washroom, about two yards wide by three yards long, with a ceiling four yards up. The walls were all concrete. The lower two yards of the walls were painted sky blue, and the upper two yards and the ceiling were white.

Two old rusty sinks stood side by side against one wall; they didn't work. A couple of wooden chairs were in place next to the sinks. To the side was a blue plastic bucket with a lid, which was to be my toilet. There was a hardback third grade Russian reader in the room, and its pages served as toilet tissue.

On one end of the room was a locked door connecting to the main hall. On the other end was another locked door leading to another room that imprisoned another captive. Heavy padlocks secured these doors, and the jihadis needed to have the key to enter my room.

Above the second door were two small windows, and light came through them from the other room, which had a lot of sunlight. My room was semi-dark in the daytime and pitch dark at night. Although it was November, the room was not too cold or damp. Nor was the air musty. On the floor was a vent from a heating system, and semi-fresh air would come into the room. It was not so chilly that I had to wear my coat; my flannel shirt kept me warm enough.

In the corner by the second door was a mat, a yard wide by two long. The cotton inside the mat wasn't evenly distributed, and some of the cloth lay right against the red brick floor. The rug was only about an inch thick where there was cotton. I promptly noted how uncomfortable the lumpy mat was, but immediately sat on it anyway and continued to pray—I knew I was in terrible danger. As time passed, I spent a lot of time on the mat, sitting or lying down while regularly praying to God.

Instinctively I understood that I needed God's help! I came to think of the dark little washroom as my ark of protection. Danger and death was outside Noah's ark during the flood, but they were safe inside the ark. I realized that Noah and others aboard did not have light in their rooms either.

Up until the New Year, my usual food server was a captor that I named "Nice." He did not use violence on me. They served us captives food three times a day *if* there was gas to operate the stove in the kitchen. Usually there was. But after a few weeks, they only served food twice a day.

Our food came in large aluminum cans, half or a third full. My diet consisted of macaroni and a hunk of white bread. Rarely, at breakfast we had a substance like cream of wheat. It looked like dog food but did not taste that bad. The water I drank seemed safe, and I could have more water if I asked for it. However, I usually did not request anything or want to attract any attention. I just tried to be a polite hostage and not stir up problems.

I learned to move quickly to the required position when people came in. They generally did not knock but just barged in. I would kneel with my face in the corner and thank the food server, trying to be submissive. Once I accidentally looked when Nice came in. Somehow, I got confused, and was sitting in the corner looking at him.

"Do that again and I will cut your head off," he said.

Nice was pure Chechen. He had dark coloring, and he wasn't tall or exceptionally muscular—like a lot of my captors at the outpost. There was rarely chatting with him when he appeared with the food.

Sometimes a different jihadi would serve my food. I named him "Kicker" because he loved to kick me. While I was hunched in the corner, he'd kick me as he was leaving the room. Kicker clearly hated me. He was the most active one in the outpost, constantly walking or running around talking about me, trying to get feedback from the other jihadis. He was a rabble rouser; he enjoyed trying to stir up trouble.

For many nights after my arrival, I did not have a candle or matches, so I ate rapidly by the little light that came through the window when my imprisoned neighbor next door had his candle lit. We always had supper after nightfall because it got dark early at this time of year. I sat on the mat while I ate, using a wooden chair as my table.

Enough light came into my room for me to get a feel for the time of day. I would wake up early and start praying. I would pray, listen, meditate—all mixed in together. Breakfast came around 10 a.m., and supper was about 4 p.m. I tried to keep track of the passing days, at first by counting them with paper shaped into numbers for dates. Later on, I used match sticks. I hid them under the mat.

At the beginning of my imprisonment, I did physical activities and little routines related to health and hygiene. In the washroom, I would use the hardback cover of the Russian reader to scrape the brick floor clean of fallen bread crumbs and dirt, and then dump the pile in my toilet bucket. I did this once a day during the daylight hours.

Most of the time, I did not have fingernail clippers, so as my nails grew I took off one nail each day with my teeth. Once the jihadis started giving me match sticks, I used those to clean my nails: after burning, the sticks would have a sharp end where the flame had been. My beard and hair just grew and grew—unimpeded.

In the first few weeks, I performed calisthenics faithfully. I did some pushups and other exercises, but I soon started to experience a real fatigue and weakness settling into my body because of the diet. I also noticed, after my first two or three weeks, that my joints creaked as I moved. I could feel myself weakening, so I stopped doing the exercises.

The time I had spent exercising became more prayer time. From the moment the Chechens first had me in the jeep on the country road, it was obvious my situation was one of spiritual warfare. After all, even Hassan had said the spiritual was the most important.

The jihadis were constantly having discussions about me. They would go off to a room and confer about what to do with me. I got to know their schedule, I became aware when they had their meetings, and these were the times I would really pray and call out to God for His divine hand of protection.

The outpost was run in a military manner, and the jihadis usually wore khaki green uniforms. They held several captives in the building, so they had a lot of their comrades watching each of us, serving food, cleaning up, and performing other military barracks-type chores. They all shared and slept in rooms surrounding mine.

One time a jihadi put his knife blade on my neck. Another time, as I was on all fours, I was told to reach out and touch a rifle. The man asked me what it was, and I replied, "A rifle." He then retorted, "To kill you with."

At three different times jihadis pointed their pistol at my face. They would walk in and say, "I am going to cut off your ear" or "I am going to cut off your nose" or "I am going to cut off your hand."

I could hear through the doors and the walls, as a result realizing what was going on much of the time. The days started to roll by, and my hearing became really sharp as I sat and listened in my dark, little washroom. I heard the intermittent call to prayer throughout the city.[15] I heard cars down on the street. I heard the jihadis walking around the building, working, talking in their rooms.

Each one had a different gait, and their voices were distinctive and recognizable. Before long, I had named each captor—either by hearing someone call him or just by making up names for them like Cap, Nice, and Kicker.

---

15 The exact location of the "outpost" is still not known. Clues, however, suggest a more urban-like setting. A suburb of the capital city of Grozny, heavily damaged during the first Chechen War (1994-1996), may be a possibility, as well as a smaller city like Urus Martan, about eighteen miles southwest of Grozny. Urus-Martan was a center of rebel military operations and of Wahhabi activism at this time..

There was one surprising thing I noticed about the jihadis as they talked outside my door: they occasionally used Portuguese words and phrases interspersed with their Russian. I could hardly believe my ears at first, and thought I must be mistaken, but they kept on, and it became clear that it was actually Portuguese. Since Linda and I had spent years in Portugal and Brazil, I could understand what they were saying. They weren't speaking it for my sake, though I did tell Cap we had lived in Portugal.

In a couple rooms down the hall there was a TV, and the jihadis would sit around and watch what was on when they had spare time. The TV was on a lot, playing Middle Eastern music and a variety of different programs.

Sometime in December, I heard a man on the TV preaching strongly and emotionally for the cause of Islam, and a group of soldiers was cheering him.

"*Allah Akbar!*" they yelled in unison—Arabic for "God is great!"[16]

One night, around this same time, a large number of jihadis were running in the building. I surmised they had come to pick up weapons that were being stored at the outpost. They rushed outside, jumped into trucks and rolled off toward some combat zone, chanting "*Allah Akbar*!" This commotion happened again the following night and one other time a few days later.

Hearing the stampeding boots a couple yards away was unnerving. When all these fighters dashed by my door, all pumped up for fighting, I wanted to disappear. Clashes between the Chechens and the Russians had been increasing over the previous year, and these jihadis were probably heading out to fight with Russians soldiers.

After the First Chechen War ended, most Chechen soldiers went home, but these jihadis would not stop fighting. They hated Russia too much, and so their holy war continued. The jihadis had two main goals for kidnapping: to get ransom money and to convert the victim to jihad Islam. Kidnap victims like me could help pay for

16 Osama bin Laden was most likely the person on the TV program that the soldiers were cheering.

their war with ransom money. If kidnap victims couldn't come up with ransom money or actually convert to jihad Islam, they would likely be killed.[17]

From early on, some of my captors wanted to take me to the killing camp, called the "*lagir*." I heard them refer to this place often as they talked about whether to take me there to kill me. The camp was a place in the Chechnya mountains where they murdered and buried people who did not produce ransom money. Some of my captors did not care as much about the money: they just wanted me dead.

One morning, "Bear" worked out a deal with several of his comrades, including Hassan, to transport me there. Bear had a heavy walk and deep voice. He was the sergeant at arms, one of the leaders of the outpost. I had heard the jihadis talking about the killing camp in their meetings, and I could hear Bear's voice among the others, debating what to do with me.

I heard the preparations: they were scurrying around getting their things ready.

A jihadi named Muktá said, "It's all fueled up." The Jeep was ready to haul me off to the camp.

Bear told Kicker, "You take care of him." Kicker, apparently, was to be the one who would blow me away. I could tell he was joyful at the thought of killing me.

They came into my room to talk with me. The idea they tried to convey was that we would be at the camp a long time as they waited for the ransom money. But I knew their actual plan was to be there a few days, dispose of me, and come back. I had heard one of them say that he had been up at the camp and that it was extremely cold, meaning too uncomfortable to stay there very long during winter. They planned to dispatch me quickly so they wouldn't have to spend much time at the killing site.

---

17 The number of kidnappings have been estimated to be as high as 1,700 or more in the late 1990s. No one can say for sure, since in many instances, killing of victims took place or ransoms were covered quickly to avoid brutal death.

If I had to go, I really wanted my tennis shoes. I told them I wanted to put these shoes on before we left the outpost; and strangely, they wanted me to have them on as well. Everything else was in order to send me off, so they started looking for the shoes.

The jihadis searched through the closet. They looked around some rooms, but they couldn't find my shoes. They didn't hunt for them that long before Bear called off the search.

"This is God!" he declared.

They all stopped looking for the shoes, except Hassan. He was furious. He went wild, scouring the closets, trying to find my tennis shoes. I heard him tearing through the rooms, slamming door after door. Finally, he too quit trying to find them.

To my immediate relief, thanks to the miraculous disappearance of my tennies, the scheme to take me to the killing camp was canceled, at least temporarily. It was blessed proof to me that God was beginning to show the jihadis His power.

After this episode, some of the jihadis started thinking and wondering about me as a spiritually minded person. God was working on their minds. Others ignored this kind of possibility and still wanted to murder me. I kept hearing these potential killers plotting, but they couldn't figure out how to get to me if God were spiritually protecting me from their wrath.

--

There was always a guard sitting outside my door. My main guard was an American! His name was Moosaá, but his real name was Philip—his fellow kidnappers called him both. He constantly sat by the door of my washroom with his automatic rifle. Sometimes I could hear him cleaning the floor outside the door, sweeping and mopping. He never said anything to me, though other soldiers would come by occasionally and chat with him.

One night, I heard him talking to another American captor. "Well, you did it to yourself," Philip said to him.

It was the first time I heard Philip speak in English. He usually communicated in Russian; I could tell by his accent that he was from the western U.S. I didn't know who the other young man was, but both of these Americans were part of the Chechen kidnapping ring. The other American was getting ready to leave the outpost, and Cap came into my room to take my leather coat. Since the washroom was warm enough, I hadn't been wearing it.

"Your colleague is leaving," Cap said, referring to the second American. "He needs your coat."

Philip regularly guarded my door. I never heard or learned more about this other American fellow. Over time I came to recognize Philip's walk and voice, as I would with the rest of them. I saw him only once, when I was returning from the third floor with Cap, after working on the ransom demand. Philip stood up by the door of my room as I walked in. For the first time we saw each other, though dimly because of the darkness. His face was shadowed; he was a tall, thin young man.

IV

SAYING GOODBYE TO DAGESTAN

Linda

November 12–14, To Moscow

I didn't sleep much that first night. I never slept well when Herb was gone.

Thursday morning, November 12, bright and early, people began to hear the news of Herb's abduction. Our apartment filled with friends from around the city: from the church, the university, and other schools where we taught, stores where we shopped, and our apartment building. Even people who lived out in the villages heard about the kidnapping and kindly came to visit me.

As new arrivals walked into the entry hall, they would repeat, sincerely, "I'm so sorry." Some friends were overcome with emotion. A group of teachers we helped at one of the elementary schools visited with their husbands, and they couldn't stop tearing up.

"I can't believe this happened," several of the ladies said. "Herb came to Dagestan to help and love people. That was all he ever did." Some felt shame about such a decent, giving person being kidnapped by criminal thugs in their midst.

By midday, the house was full of people sitting around the living room and dining room, talking, sharing, and weeping. Members of our church fellowship were able to talk with all of our friends—it was a deeply blessed time for us to share our love of Jesus with Muslim friends. (In a Muslim community we had to show the love of Jesus not just talk about it, which required time and patience.)

Among the people I wanted to see one more time was a close friend named Tatiana. She had team-taught English with me at the university. In her appearance and manner Tatiana was a very lovely person: she was tall and slender, with dark hair, and she was really attractive in a classic Russian way. She was such a good person. Tatiana had always felt responsible for Herb and me, trying to protect us. She had been afraid for our safety and for herself as well.

"No matter how much we try to protect ourselves," I said, hoping to comfort her, "something could always happen, so we might as well be doing what God wants us to do in the first place." I shared with her that the only way anyone can have peace in such a troubled world is to make peace with God through Jesus Christ. I told her that Herb may have been kidnapped, but, in terms of eternity, his situation was secure.

Tatiana cried; we hugged each other, and I whispered to her that regardless of what might happen to Herb, everything was going to be okay.

Alka briefly came by to visit me. He was afraid I might think the abduction was his fault. I assured him that I knew it wasn't and told him not to worry while thanking him for everything he had done. I explained that without him, we would not have known what had happened to Herb.

Amid these many visits Christine called our team leader Phil Cantrell to talk about our return to Moscow. He reiterated the twenty-four hour deadline for us to get out of Dagestan, but we still felt like there was too much to be done in so short a time. With people pouring into the house, we were certain there was no way we could leave by nightfall. Christine asked for another week as she pleaded our case over the phone.

"We'll have people with us constantly," she stated. "We'll be inside the apartment most of the time, with our friends, and Linda will never answer the phone."

I had avoided answering the phone all that morning. Although a lot of acquaintances and newspaper people had called, someone else always answered the phone for me. Still, our team leader didn't like the idea of us spending so much extra time in Makhachkala. He and Christine, with my approval, eventually compromised with a departure on Saturday, the 14th. That would give us one extra day to get organized, at least.

Once settled on the date, we had to make arrangements to buy tickets for our flight to Moscow. I went back to our bedroom and was getting some money together when I remembered a seeming mistake Herb had made—getting too much cash out of the bank. Here was another indication to me that God knew ahead of time what was going to happen to Herb back on Wednesday, the 11th.

That afternoon, Herb rushed into the apartment with a pile of money he had exchanged from dollars to rubles. It was a lot of money, about a thousand dollars.

"Why did you exchange so much?" I asked.

"We need the cash for the trip coming up," he explained. "We'll have to buy those tickets soon."

"Yes, but those tickets won't cost this much."

He had indeed exchanged too much money. I was complaining about the error even as Herb had gathered up his sports bag and headed out of the house for his basketball lesson at the orphanage.

"We'll think of some use for the money," he said, before disappearing down the stairwell.

Some use was right! The extra money was just the amount required to buy two tickets to Moscow. These rubles were like a gift and provision for our immediate needs from the Lord—and also from Herb! Since it was not safe for me to go out to exchange money, here in my hand was exactly what we needed to purchase our tickets.

There was something like this daily—something God did to give me peace and to make His presence obvious during these trying days.

On Friday, one of our friends arranged for a local Dagestani TV station to interview me. I agreed, if Tatiana would sit with me while I did the interview, in case I needed any help with my Russian. The interview seemed like a good idea to me for two reasons: first, the people of Makhachkala could hear me say how much we loved them and had enjoyed living here; second, the people who had kidnapped Herb might see this program, realize we were not rich, maybe feel compassion, and release him from his captivity.

Two men from the station arrived at our apartment. They were pleasant; they tried to be careful with their questions. We filmed the interview in the living room, sitting across from all our visitors, with the big cameras and lights shining on me. Tatiana sat nearby, off to the side so she wasn't in view of the camera. As matters turned out, I didn't need to ask her any questions, but her nearness gave me confidence in my use of Russian.

The interviewers asked several questions: why Herb and I moved to Dagestan, what we were doing here, whether or not we were happy with our lives in Makhachkala. Finally, they asked if there was anything I wanted to say to the people of Dagestan.

I wanted them to know how meaningful our time with them was for us, how much kindness they had shown us, and that I knew the kidnapping wasn't their fault. Our purpose was only to help spread God's Word, not for any form of personal gain, and we had fallen in love with them in the process.

"Herb isn't a rich man financially," I concluded, "but he is rich spiritually."

--

Our final evening in Dagestan, Christine and I decided to go to a meeting with all the people from our church. Some friends urged me not to go outside the apartment, but I really wanted to have a time of prayer and worship with them. A small group traveled with us, for security as we went to another church member's apartment.

Our church fellowship group was waiting in the apartment when we arrived. The big living room was full of people sitting around on couches, chairs, and the floor. There was a strong family atmosphere, enhanced by a sense of unity that became stronger after Herb's kidnapping.

The room was typical Dagestani style: Red carpets hung on the wall, and large carpets in bright blue, red, and black covered the wooden floors. Our hostess was an art teacher at the university, a sweet woman with dark hair and big brown eyes. Her home reflected her artistic tastes; it was adorned with small paintings and sculptures. The lights were dim, as they were in most homes in Dagestan.

There was a sense of sadness and uncertainty among the group because Christine and I were leaving, but there was also a spirit of thankfulness and love. "We love you all so much," I said, fighting back tears. "We wouldn't leave if we hadn't been strongly advised to go. . . . I'm leaving, but Herb is still here. . . ."

We actually didn't know where Herb was, but I was sure that he was alive—perhaps even incarcerated nearby. "Keep your eyes on Jesus and run your race, the one He has set before you," I challenged them. "We each have a different race before us: you, me, Herb, Christine but we each one have to run it with our eyes fixed on Jesus and in His strength. Keep living for His glory," I ended.

Timur gestured that he had something to add.

"We realize now that Herb was willing to give his life for us," he said. "It was a sacrifice for him. But we want you to know that it is our task to be willing to give our lives to reach our own Dagestani people with the good news of Jesus."

A few people around the room responded, "Amen," affirming what he had declared.

We sang, prayed together, and took communion. Preparing to leave, Christine and I went around to each person, hugging and reminding them that we loved them and would be praying for them. I had no doubts that they would continue to grow in their love for the Lord and for each other after we were gone. Having said goodbye, we walked out into the cold, heading for home. I knew I would never forget their sweet tear-streaked faces.

It was our last night in Makhachkala, and Christine had to go back to her apartment to pack. She hadn't left my side since Herb was abducted, not even to go home and change clothes. Marat went with her, to help and to make sure she was safe.

It was quiet and calm in our apartment. I went into the bedroom to pack a suitcase and a carry-on case. It was difficult, because without Herb I didn't feel like I needed anything. Rather, I felt like I only needed him. I pulled out our picture albums and photos of our children, our grandson, and our Dagestani friends, making sure those were packed first in the big suitcase. I also packed some nice new clothes Herb had recently received—it made me feel closer to him to have his clothes with me—and a few of my own most comfortable clothes. I threw in my Bible, some vitamins and cosmetics, Herb's new Walkman and some tapes into the carry-on.

There was nothing else I needed. I didn't want to have stress over objects that didn't matter. I told everyone in the church that I was leaving everything in our apartment to them, so they could give items to anyone who had need, or they could sell them and use the money or just give them away. I set aside my educational books and tapes to give to the university since it had very few English materials of its own.

Early Saturday morning, people arrived to say their final goodbyes. Tatiana came from the university, and I gave her the books for the university. Our church group rented a bus to take us to the Makhachkala airport. Everyone, including Tatiana, stood in a circle, held hands and prayed. It was difficult to say goodbye. About thirty people clambered aboard the rickety old bus. The driver was a nice man; we had rented his bus before, usually for church outings and for baptisms down at the Caspian Sea.

The airport was a modest facility. The main building had a front room with counters for check-in and small concession stands selling snack food nearby; and there was one room in the rear. Our big jet plane was sitting out back on the tarmac reminding me of a large rigid bird.

We piled into the airport. The church people came with us into the waiting room, walking right past the document check-in like they were supposed to be there. They stayed with us, and we waited until the last possible minute.

It was so hard to leave. For the first time, I was stronger than Christine. She had a difficult time making it through the final security check and walking through the door leading outside. All of our friends from the church stood at the door, waving, watching us leave.

It was cold and clear outside, but we could barely see anything. The tears were streaming down our faces, and we could hardly see the plane as we walked along, hanging on to each other. Christine couldn't speak. She was being forced to leave with me simply because no other missionaries from TEAM were currently in Makhachkala—or even Dagestan—at that particular time. She was such a good missionary, loving the Dagestanis and having a wonderful way of sharing the love of Jesus with them.

My heart was aching, realizing that I was leaving behind Herb, everyone I loved in Makhachkala, and my life's missionary work. Our years there had been an exciting time of ministry time with unreached people who were so responsive—a fulfilling experience in such a special way…now over and likely forever gone. Even though the door was shutting for us in Dagestan, the Lord was comforting me with peaceful feelings. There was no frustration or anger, just sadness, the sensation of leaving our missionary work undone and grief over that great loss, especially since I sensed that I would never again return to Dagestan.

As the plane took off, I looked out the little window next to my seat. "Goodbye, Herb," I whispered. "God—please take care of him." I watched until the airport and city faded from my sight as we began flying northwestward toward Moscow.

V

SEEKING ASSISTANCE IN MOSCOW

Linda

November 14–18, Key Meetings

It seemed like a long, long flight to Moscow....

We were met at the Sheremetyevo Airport in Moscow by our mission colleagues. To see friends immediately when we got off the plane was very comforting. They did not know what to say to me, but they warmly hugged me, which was exactly what I needed. Christine and I acted as if we were doing okay, as much as possible under the circumstances.

Our colleagues helped us pull our suitcases off the old, broken carousel, and they led us outside to a taxi stand. We rode in a rickety cab to the apartment of an older couple who taught at the missionary school in Moscow. Herb and I had stayed with them when we visited the capital earlier that year. Reaching this apartment was like going to a quiet farmhouse in the country: It was peaceful, serene, cozy, decorated with crocheted throw rugs and little objects from America.

The couple had a meal ready for us when we arrived. Everyone was concerned that I wasn't eating enough. Truthfully, I had to fight to eat. My stomach felt like it had a rock in the bottom of it.

Waiting for me in Moscow was another gift from the Lord that reminded me of His ever-present love. It was a package from a missionary friend who had recently published a new book. Herb and I often had mail directed to us via a TEAM address in Moscow before someone delivered it to us in Dagestan. The book was *The Perfect Love* by Ruth Myers—one of the first copies, and the Lord used it to calm my heart and to speak of His infinite love for me.[18]

"Perfect love" was God's love. There was something uplifting about opening this package. I didn't know Ruth had authored the book, and I had no idea this copy had arrived in Moscow, but here it was—waiting for me. It was as if God was saying, "I knew you'd be coming . . . here is a very special message for you."

In the afternoon, Dave Davis, our area director from TEAM, flew in from the states to Moscow, and we had the opportunity to talk.[19] Dave was a tall man, with close-cropped salt and pepper hair and glasses perched in front of his twinkling eyes, though his eyes were now filled with tears. We sat in our hosts' living room and talked about what we could do, even though we knew so few details about Herb's kidnapping.

"I'm so sorry this happened," Dave said. "I promise we'll do everything possible to help get Herb released."

There was so much unknown. No one had yet claimed to have Herb, and we had no idea where he might be, if prayerfully still alive. No missionary from TEAM had ever been kidnapped before—this was a new experience for all of us.

Dave had brought another person with him who did have experience in crisis situations. Our mission would have to support the American and Russian authorities with negotiations, since the U.S. and Russian governments each had a no-ransom money policy. They thought it was necessary to discourage future kidnappings.

---

18 See Ruth Myers, *The Perfect Love: Intensely Personal, Overflowing, Never Ending* (Colorado Springs, Colorado: WaterBrook Press, 1998). The official publication date was June 1, 1998.

19 Dave Davis was based at TEAM headquarters in Illinois and had administrative responsibilities watching over TEAM activities in Europe and western Asia. Earlier he had served as a missionary in Pakistan.

If missions and governments regularly paid ransoms, many more people would be abducted for money.

"Hostage negotiations are a complicated process," this adviser explained. "But we'll help do what's necessary for your husband's release."[20]

Everything was overwhelming to me.

"Please, I only have one husband," I said, trying not to cry. "Please help us."

I realized after we finished speaking that Herb's abduction was also a real trauma for TEAM. As I sat there and poured out my heart to Dave, I was just adding more pressure. I knew Dave cared greatly about Herb: he'd been our area director for many years, including while we were working in Portugal. Dave was distressed about Herb's disappearance and was stressed and frazzled in thinking about the task before him.

We prayed together for Herb's safety and for wisdom. Our mission colleagues from Moscow came over and joined us in our hosts' apartment to pray, to talk about the kidnapping and how they might help.

I felt as if I were in a dream world. I wanted to say to Dave and the others who would be working with the governments that my primary hope was really in the Lord. I did not want them to feel pressure from me to attempt to do humanly what, in reality, only God could accomplish.

--

We continued our weekend wait in Moscow until our meeting at the American embassy on Monday, the 16th. With some free time on Sunday, Christine and I attended an uplifting church service.... After the service was over, a young Russian gentleman stood up at the podium and asked for prayer requests. Someone who knew about Herb's kidnapping sent a note up to this man, mentioning my attendance. He invited me to come up front should I want to

20 This person, sometimes referred to as the "crisis adviser," has not been identified.

share a little. I nodded and walked forward to tell those present what was happening.

"It isn't out of God's control," I stated. "He will be standing with Herb through it all. Please pray that God's will shall be done, and that the Lord will take care of Herb and protect him from harm in every way, for God's greater glory."

Returning to my seat, I felt a tap on my shoulder. Behind me was a short, young woman with light brown hair. "I had an experience I'd like to share with you," she said. "I think it might be encouraging."

The young woman's family had recently been living in Chechnya. She related how she had been taken prisoner by the police, along with her parents and sister. These abductors were after ransom money. Somehow, they were all released except her sister. The captors had tried to kill her several times, but they kept botching their attempts. One time, they stood her sister up to be executed by gunshot, but the gun didn't work. They finally let her sister go, at which point her family fled to Moscow.

The young woman encouraged me by saying that God possessed the power to take care of Herb, as He had her sister, and that God would be able to get him released. She said that she would be constantly praying for Herb. I thanked her, glad she shared with me. Her story really lifted my spirits.

After we were done speaking, a young American missionary came up to me. "I have a question for you," he said. "Do you really think you were supposed to be in Dagestan? Do you think it was God's will for you to be there?"

I thought about these questions for a few moments and then replied, with certainty, "Yes, I do. I am sure we were in exactly the right place at the right time."

Were we in the wrong place? No.

"God's ways are often not our ways," I told one young missionary then resident in Moscow, "God is sovereign, and He's busy doing something.

I am convinced that He will bless and protect Herb somehow, some way, in the ordeal we are now facing—and well beyond."

I also stated to him that I was thankful that Herb and I had given all of our adult lives to sharing the love of Jesus with those who didn't yet know about His miraculous powers.

"I wouldn't change one minute of all those years," I said, "even right up to this moment. Helping to save the souls of people is worth any cost."

The young missionary smiled and replied, "Well, I'll be praying for you. Please try to keep in touch."

"I'll definitely try" was my heartfelt response.

--

I had additional free time that Sunday afternoon. I read a book called *The Secret Invasion*, about a Danish pastor who risked his life many times to get the gospel of Jesus into countries where Bibles were not allowed. The Lord miraculously helped him avoid many close encounters with death.[21]

Later in the afternoon I was meditating on *The Secret Invasion* and on the cost of ministry in Dagestan. I knew that God would work things out for the furtherance of the gospel and for His glory. In many ways, it was safer to be an American residing there than it was being a president of Dagestan, who had been shot at many times.[22] Amid so much chaos, we hadn't carefully considered the threat of kidnapping, a large issue regarding personal security in

21 Hans Kristian and Dave Hunt, *The Secret Invasion* (Eugene Oregon: Harvest House Publishers, 1987).

22 Magomedali Magomedov served as the president of Dagestan from 1992 to 2006. A self-serving political moderate, he apparently dodged assassination attempts. Not so with the highly corrupt mayor of Makhachkala, Said Amirov, who was in office from 1998 to 2013. He had numerous enemies and survived an estimated fifteen assassination attempts. In 1993, one such incident left him with a damaged spine and confined to a wheel chair. In 1998, he survived two more efforts to blow him up. One in early September involved a bomb that exploded too soon near his home and killed twenty neighbors along with another eight wounded. This failed attempt unleashed a wave of violence all through the streets of the capital city and helped to spark sectarian violence in the Muslim community.

Dagestan. We knew that we could be physically hurt or even killed, but we kept our focus on why the Lord had us living in Makhachkala for a reason—the critical importance of spreading His gospel in untouched corners of the world.

"If God is leaving this door open," Herb said, "I'll walk through it. And if God would allow my life to be taken, so be it."

Two and a half months earlier, Herb and I had left Makhachkala at the request of the national leadership of TEAM. They'd put us on a train to Moscow because an Islamic leader had been killed at a mosque by what appeared to be jihadi extremists—he was blown up for not being fanatical enough.[23]

As a result, many men in Makhachkala armed themselves with guns and were angrily roaming the city—moderate believers against extremists. Our local church leaders told us to leave until they thought we could return safely, arguing, "There's no reason for you to get hit by a bullet from local feuding that doesn't involve you."

Herb had such a strong passion for evangelism, though his primary concern was for me and our close friend Christine, not for himself. He didn't want us to return to Makhachkala if either she or I felt unsafe in any way. We agreed that if our national leaders believed going back was safe enough, as they did within a few weeks, we should return, as we did. Our determination was to keep moving forward with our missionary work.

Once we were back in Dagestan, the Spirit of God put our activity in the church on fast forward. Small groups began to organize more effectively, and group leaders enjoyed being discipled by Herb. Local Dagestanis took almost all the responsibility for activities in the church, and the Good News was spreading that our bonds of unity and love were being strengthened. God did so much, so quickly during these last few weeks in Makhachkala. We marveled at the work of the Lord in our midst.

And then Herb was abducted.

23 Most likely radical Muslim Wahabis were responsible for this killing of a more moderate Islamic leader.

--

Christine and I were more than ready for our appointment at the American embassy on Monday morning. We were told that we would meet with the Consul General for a few minutes before someone from the consulate would accompany me to an interview with the Moscow police.

Snow had fallen—dirty snow was piled everywhere—so our taxi took quite a while to maneuver through the busy downtown streets on our way to the embassy.

We walked up toward the main door of the embassy and told the Marine guard standing there that we had an appointment at the consulate.

"You are at the wrong entrance," he indicated. "This door is only for people getting passports and visas."

"How do we get in to see the Consul General?"

He pointed down the street and said, "Go around that way. There's an entrance on the other side."

We set off walking through the snow and cold. The embassy was a large complex with big buildings surrounded by a high stuccoed security wall. We followed the wall, walking along the street as cars whizzed past. About a half-mile later, after taking wrong turns twice, we arrived at the correct gate. Our appointment was soon, and we tried to hurry, but the guard refused to let us in until we showed him our passports. Finally, we reached the security desk.

A young Marine in uniform stood at a desk behind the window. He was very formal.

"We have an appointment with the Consul General," I stated. I was tired from our long, cold walk.

The Marine looked at us doubtfully.

"What's your name?"

"Linda Gregg."

He pulled out a clipboard and scanned a list of names with appointment times.

"Sorry, but your name isn't on the list," he said curtly, before walking away from the window.

By now, we were actually late for our meeting. Despite my resolve, tears started rolling down my cheeks.

Christine was furious. She called the young Marine back to the opening of the window, beckoning firmly with her finger.

"What do you mean her name isn't on the list? This woman's husband has just been kidnapped, and she's been through enough without such lack of courtesy at the American embassy. You'd better get your facts straight and find out that we *do* have an appointment, and you'd better act *now*!"

The Marine took off at a run. It made me laugh to see Christine so furious, and him high tailing it down the corridor. She hugged me, and we prayed that the Lord would help us get into the appointment.

In a few minutes, the Marine came back with a contrite spirit and with a tall and very pleasant lady: Laura Clerici, the Consul General. She was newly assigned to Moscow, and she was still unpacking her boxes.

"Oh, I'm so sorry for the mix-up," she said. "It's entirely my fault."

She led us through many corridors and hallways on our way to her office in another building. Laura was most gracious. She asked if we wanted something to drink as we walked by a small snack area. We sat down, and she asked a few questions about the kidnapping and whether I was okay, inquiring if there was anything she could do to help me. I liked Laura right away.

Waiting in Laura's office was her assistant: a very businesslike young woman, well dressed.[24] Laura first introduced her and then a courteous young Russian man who helped them interpret when they talked with Russian officials. The plan was for him to go with us to the Russian police station and translate for me.

Even though I could speak Russian, they said it would be faster and clearer to have him translate. I was nervous about the interview

24 Kelly Adams-Smith, chief of the American Citizens Service Center at the embassy.

and was glad to have his assistance. We met another man who was an FBI agent. He would also come with us, just to watch and listen. He was tall, with dark hair, and he wore a long trench coat.[25]

As we were ushered out the door to a waiting car, Christine whispered, "He looks like Sherlock Holmes."

This comment made me laugh again. The Lord was gracious to let me enjoy Christine's company. Her humor often broke the tension that swept in waves over me.

We were late, so we had to get on the road quickly. There was a huge black car waiting for us. It was comfortable and roomy, not like the little cars being driven down in Dagestan. The assistant seemed to know the translator, and they chatted during the drive. They explained more to me about what to expect. I was nervous, not knowing what the Russians would ask. The translator was helpful and talkative, and he obviously knew what he was doing. The FBI agent was silent throughout the drive.

At the police station, a Russian police officer met us. He took us into a room that reminded me of a small court chamber. Up front were tiered wooden desks that faced out onto a few rows of wooden chairs. A woman sat where a judge would be located. Several other police officers, all wearing brownish green uniforms, sat a little below and to the right of the policewoman.

We were led to the first row of chairs facing the officers. The set up was formidable. I noted how dissimilar it was from the run down Dagestani police station.[26]

The translator introduced me, and one of the police officers launched into a series of questions about who Herb and I were. He sat right in front of me, and he appeared to be the official question-asker. The policewoman said nothing. A policeman on the far side was taking notes. Even though I understood the man's

25 James Treacy, the assistant legal attaché then serving at the embassy.

26 Linda was meeting with police officers working for the Russian Ministry of Internal Affairs' Organized Crime Unit. The Russians took the lead through a special agent named "Mr. K" in negotiating Herb's release agreement.

questions, I let the translator tell me about the question in English. I responded in English, and the translator repeated my answer in Russian. It took longer, but I appreciated having the extra time to consider my answers.

"What were you doing in Dagestan?" the police officer asked. He was sneering slightly and seemed to be a little angry.

"We were teaching English at the university and at an elementary school, helping at an orphanage, and training teachers at a continuing education institute. . . ." I listed off many of our jobs and ministries.

"Who invited you? Who gave you your visas?"

The policeman's demeanor seemed to darken as he asked more questions.

"Didn't you know it was dangerous in Dagestan?" he asked.

"We understood the risks," I answered, "but neither the Russians nor the U.S. embassy told us we shouldn't be there."

"Why, if you knew it was dangerous, did you go down to Dagestan and stay there?"

I grew tired of the policeman's belligerent attitude. I forgot to wait for the translator and immediately answered the question in Russian.

"We went down there to help people," I said. I looked determinedly right at the police officer. "Yes, it is dangerous, but just because it was dangerous doesn't mean the needs go away. There is such an incredible need, and nobody cares about them! You Russians don't care. You know that Russians think Dagestan is the armpit of Russia. Nobody wants to help these people! But we absolutely fell in love with them… so much so that we were probably blinded to the possible dangers that were swirling all around us."

I couldn't believe I had spoken so boldly. The policeman's face softened; he cleared his throat. Other police up front shifted behind their desks. The man then asked some generic questions about the Dagestani police, but his attitude had definitely changed. My translator motioned that it was okay for me to continue answering the questions myself.

When the interview was over, the policewoman walked up to me. She appeared to be the captain, or at least the person in charge. I thanked her and told her my hope was in the Lord.

She hugged me and said, "I have been praying since I heard about your husband's abduction, and I will continue to pray for you. But you must return to the U.S. soon because the people who have Herb will try to contact you. "You are the weakest link," she said, "because you care more than anyone else involved. If they do make contact, they will make a demand; and if they make a demand you cannot meet, they will have to hurt Herb to show how serious they are."

She handed me some papers to sign, which gave them permission to work on getting Herb released, and she said, "We will do everything possible to free your husband."

We hugged again and our small group filed out of the building and into the big car to drive back to the American embassy. The translator said I had done a good job. The FBI agent still didn't say anything.

At the embassy, Christine and I followed Laura's assistant James Treacy into a large conference room. Sitting around the room were Dave Davis, our team leader, the crisis adviser, Laura, and a few other people. They were in the middle of a conversation when our group entered. Once introduced to everyone, they advised me to return to my home in the States and not answer any telephone calls from the kidnappers. I responded that we would be leaving for the U.S. on Wednesday.

"We will be working with the Russian government and your mission organization," Laura said. "We will take care of things and work toward getting Herb released."

The U.S. ambassador to Russia, James F. Collins, popped into the room. He was wearing a sharp gray suit and looked to be a very busy man.[27] He approached me and shook my hand.

"I am so sorry," he said. "We'll do everything we can to get your husband out of captivity."

I thanked him. He was very kind to take the time both to greet and reassure me.

"I really appreciate your help and everything you can do," I said to Ambassador Collins, and everyone also present there. "However, you should know that my real hope is in the Lord."

I thought of Psalm 62:5-7: *My soul, wait silently for God alone, for my expectation is from Him . . . . The rock of my strength, and my refuge, is in God.* These words weren't something I said just to be saying; I really felt them with my whole heart. I knew quite possibly God would direct the actions of every person here, along with the Russian police, but I knew that He was the one in charge of every detail involving Herb's situation.

As we departed, I shook hands with each person, thanking them for their assistance. At that point, James Treacy, the silent FBI agent, moved toward me.

"The Lord is able," he said, shaking my hand.

I thanked him, secretly amazed. His statement touched my heart and created an important bond.

Once finished at the embassy, Christine and I returned to our hosts' apartment. A good friend there wanted to take us out for a fun supper, in part to celebrate being done with the official business. We went to a place called the American Bar and Grill—one of Herb's and my favorite places to eat in Moscow. They made delicious American-style hamburgers. The restaurant was decorated in a Western cowboy style with sawdust all over the floor.

We sat at a square wooden table, ordered our hamburgers, and chatted happily until the waitress served our food. I looked down

27 James F. Collins, an experienced and well-respected diplomat, received the appointment as the U. S. Ambassador to Russia from President Bill Clinton in 1997 and served in that post until 2001.

at my plate and suddenly felt terrible. I couldn't eat or drink as I sat, staring at the food with tears in my eyes.

"Here I am," I thought, "enjoying something like this when Herb is being held somewhere, hopefully still alive and barely with any food at all!"

I was struck by the polar difference in our circumstances. I prayed silently for Herb, that he would have decent food to eat, and somehow I realized that Herb would never want me not to have something simply because he was forced to go without it. Christine asked me what was disturbing me. I told them my thoughts. Christine responded: "I'm sure Herb would be relieved to know that you're okay and are able to have this treat." I nodded and ate the hamburger for Herb.

--

Wednesday, November 18, dawned—exactly one week after Herb had been kidnapped. We were about to leave Moscow for America. The thought of traveling thousands of miles away from Herb was very unsettling, not quite as painful as leaving Dagestan, but almost as bad.

I had only my carry-on case and the one suitcase, which held some of Herb's clothes. Believing in God's power to free him, I left one set of Herb's clothes at our hosts' apartment for him to use when released from captivity.

Joined by Dave Davis, we soon set out for the airport in a taxi. I was quiet, lost in my thoughts, staring out the window as the taxi made its way through the congested streets of Moscow. The city seemed cold and ugly. Piles of dirty snow covered the street corners. The dark, cloudy day matched my spirit perfectly.

When we reached the airport, Christine and I prayed before we passed into the departure area. We asked the Lord to take care of Herb, our dear friends in Makhachkala, and all those working on Herb's release. We asked that God's will would be accomplished through them, and also through our lives as we resided in the distant United States.

The Sheremetyevo Airport was crowded with people, hundreds of passengers traveling to a lot of different places. I looked at the people going merrily on their way and wished they knew what a horrible event had happened in my life. It was weird to be surrounded by so many people whose lives were normal, when my life was overwhelmingly not normal.

My emotions tumbled over each other, as I had never returned to the U. S. without being really happy with the thought of seeing family and friends. For years, every time we returned home, we felt like kissing the ground. Now, my thoughts were about leaving Herb behind and how I might never be able to return to Russia, let alone Dagestan. The uncertainty and the disconnection was an awful thought—detaching from my husband, our work, our ministry, our friends in Makhachkala, and our missionary team.

Deep sadness described my feelings. My image was like that of jumping off a cliff or walking out into the unknown, even though secure in my faith that God Almighty was there and that He would guide and keep us firmly fixed in the palm of His hand during the coming days of trial. Yes, I was in free fall, but I knew His strong arms would constantly hold, guide, and uplift me.

Walking through the final gate onto the waiting plane was a struggle. Goodbye to Herb was my thought, but not goodbye forever. With reluctance and tears glistening in our eyes, Christine and I boarded the plane and were soon in the air over Moscow, now accepting the reality of continuing our undesired journey back to the United States.

VI

ENDURING THE TRIBULATIONS OF MY CAPTIVITY

Herb

Late November Into December, the Outpost

Nearing the end of November, Cap came in and told me we were soon going to make a video recording. He sat down on one of the wooden chairs and instructed me regarding what to say, all in Russian. I had to memorize phrases to get the exact content right. It was daunting to me, because my Russian wasn't that good, certainly not fluent. I rehearsed my spiel constantly so I would not botch it up.

A few days later, on Friday, November 27, Cap returned for me.[28] We walked to a large, empty classroom on the third floor, and I sat down on a mat by the wall. Cap had the camcorder, and one or two other captors were in the room, watching. All of them wore terrorist head coverings that had holes for their eyes and noses so I couldn't see their faces.

Cap had me relate to him what I was going to say, and I repeated my memorized appeal for help. He wasn't happy with the message. He scrambled the words around and ordered me to say this more

28 This was the day after Thanksgiving in 1998,

frightening message. In response, I actually swooned out of fear for a few seconds. My fear was that it was beyond my capacity to speak extemporaneously into a camcorder using my very faulty Russian.

Before turning on the camcorder, Cap handcuffed me to a pipe for effect. He told me I would be a Rambo-like hero in the States when I was freed. Once he started filming, I followed Cap's orders and said how awful my situation was; how I was in a cold place and not doing well; and that the men who held me captive were serious and wanted $3.5 million for my release.

I was supposed to make my health appear worse than it was. While filming, Cap told me to take off my sock cap, so I could be seen better. There was an emphasis on urgency, on getting the money soon. It was all part of their strategy to make everything seem terrible to the viewers, and to create publicity and support for me in order to get the ransom money. I did the best I could.

After the filming, I had to write a letter to our colleague in Moscow, repeating the ransom demand. I composed the letter in Russian, but basically restated what I said in the video. Cap carefully checked over the letter when I was done.

"We will send these to your people in Moscow," he said. "Who can take it?"

Of the church people in Makhachkala, the only phone number I could remember was for Timur and Marat's family, because I had called them all the time. I suggested Cap find a way to get the cassette to them.

"Is there any place by your apartment where we could drop off the tape?" Cap asked.

"There's an electrical box on the wall outside our front door," I replied. "That might be a good place to put the cassette."

This location had immediately come to mind: in the stairwell of our apartment building, on every landing, there were big electrical boxes with covers and lots of wires. Those areas were always a mess and poorly lit—good places to hide things.

Cap called the abductors who initially nabbed me off the street and had them look around my apartment area. They discovered that the electrical box on the floor below ours was most suitable. Cap sent the cassette and the letter to these cohorts in crime, and they stashed it in the box. Marat then picked these items up. Timur carried them to my colleagues in Moscow, who made copies to share with the Russian authorities.

Cap was the kidnapper jihadi directly in charge of me. He was also the telephone and money man at the outpost. He would call relatives and friends of the prisoners and lay out the kidnappers' money demands.

Within a few days of my arrival at the outpost, Cap came into my room and asked who he could contact about my ransom.

"Give me telephone numbers," he pressed.

I could only think of a few, those I had called frequently: Timur's family, my colleague Phil Cantrell, another friend in Moscow, and my daughter Amy's number in the States.

"These are what I can recall," I said. "I don't specifically remember any others."

I kept trying to cooperate fully. The best posture, I decided, was to remain docile, to comply with their demands and submit to everything they said, except in compromising my Christian faith.

--

Cap had a lot of experience with kidnap victims, so he could tell that I was trying hard to cooperate. He was pleased about getting the phone numbers. He appreciated my efforts, and he did not mistreat me for many weeks.

Several days after we made the video, Cap and I called my colleague in Moscow, Phil Cantrell, our regional team leader. We were in the large third floor classroom again, with a cell phone. My colleague was trying to determine if it was really me on the phone.

"Is that you, Herb?"

"Yes, it's me."

Phil sounded as if he wasn't sure.

"Do you have a Bible?" he asked.

When Cap overheard this, he got angry. He grabbed the cell phone out of my hand and berated my colleague, calling the Bible nonsense –"*yeroondá*." He insisted we converse in Russian, rather than English, so he could understand what we were saying. He also demanded that I state that my health was really getting bad, and that my colleague should hurry up his efforts to get the ransom money.

"Where was your honeymoon?" Phil asked. He still wasn't certain it was me, so he asked a question that only I could answer.

But I just blanked. I couldn't remember where Linda and I had honeymooned!! Too late, I remembered it had been at Pacific Grove.

"Um, I can't recall the exact spot . . ."

The pitch of my voice also had gone up because I was fatigued. I'd spoken with my colleague on the phone and in person many times, but he was not used to hearing the change in my voice when I was really tired. Phil didn't believe it was me.

"Is that really you, Herb?"

"Yes, it's me."

He kept on asking if it was really me. I assured him with a chuckle that it really was; it struck me as funny that he apparently thought it was someone else, clearly not trusting my Chechen captors.

Chuckling was the wrong thing to do.

Cap again grabbed the phone and shouted that he was going to kill me if my colleague did not cooperate. Cap abruptly ended the conversation and cut off the phone call. He grabbed my neck and squeezed my throat, reiterating that he was going to kill me. I was surprised and shocked.

"What do you think this is—a hotel?" He acted really mad and chewed me out for making it seem as though I was enjoying kind treatment. His strategy required me to say I was in extremely bad surroundings while sounding sick and miserable. Chuckling was not a part of his strategy.

Cap took his hand off my throat with a huff and marched across the room, leaving me alone.

"Well, I tried to help," I said to him. "I didn't think fast enough . . ."

I tried to give some excuse, to show him that I was honestly trying to cooperate.

Cap's anger with me was mostly a mock form of rage. He was a real actor, though I briefly thought otherwise when he squeezed my throat. He was good at manipulating, since he was intelligent and experienced in getting ransom payments for hostages. As for me, I was learning his tricks and how the system worked at the jihadi outpost.

--

I was the first American abducted by these Chechen jihadis. Cap would call my colleague and get nowhere with his games. As such, Cap became more willing to try talking on the phone to other people. At one point, we switched to calling Timur's family. It was a blessing I could remember their number. I don't know what I would have done without that contact, since Marat and Timur were able to pick up the video cassettes and take copies to the Russian investigators.

Several times I was with Cap when he made calls. We would go upstairs to the big classroom and use his cell phone. He definitely wanted me with him whenever he called my daughter's house in the States. One time, Amy answered the phone. Cap said, "*Alo*," but he couldn't talk to her in English. She hung up immediately. Amy knew who it was and had been instructed not to speak with my captors.

"Who was that?" Cap asked me.

"That was my daughter," I replied.

Cap was surprised to find out that I would always tell him the truth about my family. As he was able to confirm bits of such information that I shared, his opinion of me started to soften.

Cap worked with other prisoners at the outpost in negotiating for ransom money. He would tromp through my room to talk to Magamed—Russian for *Mohammed*. "Maga" was the prisoner in the room on the other side of mine, the space that had light. Cap would talk with him about as often as he would talk with me. Over time, I overheard many conversations between Cap and Maga.

Maga was an Avar, the largest ethnic group of Dagestan, and he was already at the outpost when I arrived. He was probably in his twenties; he had also lived in Makhachkala.

We never spoke. We didn't dare try—one time caught talking would have been enough for us to lose our heads—but we learned about each other's lives because we listened to these conversations through the door.

They would talk about Islam. Cap tried to persuade Maga to believe in jihad and to get him to convert. At first, Maga was noncommittal; he wouldn't say anything about this subject.[29]

One day, I heard Cap say $100,000, so I guessed this was the ransom figure needed to free Maga. They talked about money, and Cap insisted Maga's relatives could raise that sum. Cap was almost insanely severe and belligerent, and I felt sorry for Maga.

Both he and I were powerless against Cap, in the sense that we did not want to anger him. Several different times, the two of them would be conversing about money or Islam, and Cap would have some sort of tirade. He went on and on, speaking rapidly in Russian, about how Maga's family should be able to produce the money.

Cap would get started on a rampage, reprimanding Maga for not obtaining ransom funds, and Maga couldn't say anything. After two or three of these sessions, I felt really badly for him. He had to sit helplessly and silently as Cap's venomous intensity poured out over him. I was amazed that Cap could be so intense as hatred just streamed out of his mouth.

There was no real reasoning with Cap, no two-way give and take. He was a fanatic. He did have a good side, though: I could tell he liked me and did not really want to harm me. In my case, he only

29 This observation by Herb suggests that Cap was a Wahhabi fundamentalist and that Maga held more moderate beliefs. Many such captives came from local families, not known for their wealth. The fate of Maga is not known.

wanted big money for the cause of jihad. He could be pleasant, cheerful and humorous. He *was* that way with his buddies. But I never could predict when he would turn harsh and angry. I had to be very careful *what* I said to him and *how* I said it, always showing deference and respect.

Cap was Chechen, and he was serious about his chosen form of Islam and its holy war. I realized I could not say much spiritually to him or to Hassan. As the days and weeks passed at the outpost, I remained hopeful that their inflexibility would change. Regardless, I remained deeply thankful that the Lord was answering my prayers and keeping me alive while patiently enduring the tribulations of my captivity.

VII

REVELATION AND RETURNING HOME

Linda

November-December, From Moscow to Arizona

Christine and I were flying home from Moscow in a large plane, although not fully booked. We sat on the left-hand side in a two-seat section by ourselves. When the movie came on, Christine wanted to watch the film, but she couldn't see the TV screen very well from where we were sitting. She asked if I would mind her moving to a better location to watch the movie.

"Will you be all right?" she was always very conscientious.

"Yes, I'll be fine," I said, smiling and waving my hand for her not to worry. "Go watch the movie if you'd like."

Christine left for a different seat, and I sat wondering what to do with myself. I didn't feel like watching a movie, and I didn't feel like listening to the Aeroflot music channels. *Perfect Love* was with me, but I didn't feel like reading. I didn't know what to do.

I thought about what was in my carry-on. I remembered Herb's new Walkman and the tapes I'd thrown into the bag. Usually, I wouldn't use a Walkman, but the idea of listening to some Christian songs seemed soothing. Looking into my carry-on, I saw a *Praise Six* tape, one of my favorites, and decided to play this music on the Walkman.[30]

I had heard this tape dozens of times, enough that I often started humming the next tune before it began; but when I started to listen this time, it seemed like the first time I had ever heard the words. Every single song on the tape, every single word, had so much powerful meaning. The tape played the songs back and forth, automatically. Such a time of intimate worship I had never known. I became a participant in the words, not just a listener. I felt them from depths of my heart, as if I had written them.

This time was precious, as if there was a connection from God's Spirit to my spirit. This feeling was brand new to me and drew me deeper and deeper into the songs and worship. Crying, I was totally absorbed up in a deep fellowship with the Lord when an absolutely amazing experience took place. I was unprepared, having never heard or read about anything like this happening to anyone.

Suddenly, a bright light enveloped me. It wasn't like light from the sun or a light bulb or any other light I had ever known. The light was radiant. I realized that I was seeing the Lord, the actual presence of God. It wasn't frightening, but rather marvelous. My eyes weren't open, but I was seeing God face to face!

God began revealing Himself to me, one attribute after another—characteristics like His holiness, patience, mercy, righteousness, peace, goodness, and joy. This revelation from Him to me didn't involve words. The closest phenomenon I could imagine was like osmosis of cells. The knowledge of God's complete omniscience came into my mind, a kind of knowing without having to go through the English language.

The revelation between the magnificent holy God and sinful me was incredible. Feeling profoundly sorry to be such a sinner in stark contrast to His holiness, I remember doubling over weeping

30 Initially recorded in 1982, "Praise and Sing: Come and Sing Praises" featured the Maranatha Singers. Among the songs included are "Make Me a Servant," "As For Me," and "Holy, Holy, Holy."

because He allowed me in His marvelous presence even though I absolutely didn't deserve to be there.

The glory of God amazed me. Seeing Him as He is, as He *truly* is, made me feel my own shortcomings. Then, even as I was agonizing over my unworthiness, the Spirit seemed to touch my spirit and told me to remember that because of Jesus, everything was all right. Jesus paid the price on the cross for my sins, and I had accepted that act of love when I was thirteen years old. The appreciation for who He is and what He had done for me on the cross skyrocketed as I could see who He REALLY is!

The fellowship continued: a revelation of more attributes. I was still thinking over and over again, "I know me, I shouldn't be here," when into my mind the Lord whispered, "Yes, you shouldn't be here, but you're here because I love you." Waves of love started pouring over me like waves of the ocean. It was magnificent, and I felt like my heart would explode.

"Oh, God," I said. "If you don't stop, I'll die."

Immediately, three thoughts came to me in rapid succession.

"If this is the way you are," my first thought was, "it doesn't matter if you take Herb home to be with you. Please take me, too."

I was completely released from the fear of Herb's dying. I knew that God had Herb fully protected in the palm of His hand, and everything would be okay. Even if He took him, it would be okay. I was seeing a glimpse of what would be in store for Herb, and I wanted to go with him, to be with the Lord if he went. Despite the wonderful things in my life—our ministry, our children and grandchild, our friends—it all held no attraction for me at this moment. I wanted the Lord to just beam me up! Any fears I had of death were gone.

Then I thought, "Why do we cry when Christians die?"

I understood what it was to miss people and to grieve over their loss, but somehow we don't fully comprehend to the glory awaiting them, how splendid He is and how magnificent it will be for them in heaven. If we did, we would have the biggest celebrations imaginable, better than the most festive of weddings.

Finally, I thought, "Lord – this is *You*! I've been searching for you all my life, to know You like this, but I've been so wrapped up in the means to this end that I haven't gotten my gaze on You, to know You in all your magnificence."

I was busy asking God to help me to continue knowing know Him like this when I began to hear the music again. I realized that I hadn't heard the music during my amazing experience with Him. The light also began to dim. As it faded, I tried harder to focus on the songs, to keep the light and the Lord's presence, but the fading continued even as the music grew louder.

When the light left me, I recalled the experience of the martyr Stephen.

I knew—I really *knew—who* Stephen had seen when the crowd stoned him to death. I knew who the apostle Paul had seen when he was caught up into heaven. I knew who Isaiah had seen when he saw the temple filled with the Lord. And I knew who Moses had seen on Mount Sinai, when he came down from the mountain and his face radiated light.

"Oh," I thought, "my face must be shining like Moses's had shone after He saw God."

Suddenly, I realized that Christine was sitting next to me. She had been there awhile, since the movie was already over. I opened one eye and peeped at her sideways.

"Christine?"

"Linda, are you okay?" she asked. She was looking at me with curiosity.

"Christine, do you see anything with my face?"

"No," she replied, puzzled. "Your face looks okay to me."

Trying to tell her what happened was impossible. I started to explain it with words, but they were too inadequate, and I couldn't finish a sentence. It didn't make any sense. Shaking my head, I gave up.

"Well, I saw that you were crying," she observed, "but I knew you weren't crying about Herb. I could tell you were worshipping."

"Yes . . . I was worshipping!"

The experience was over, but the Lord left a deep root of strength and peace in my mind and heart, like a tree trunk thrust down into me all the way to my toes. I now had the assurance of who He was and how everything, no matter what happened, would turn out well in the end.

I looked out the window of the plane and saw the sun shining majestically through the clouds, stretching out in shades of rose and peach—a beautiful sight.

"There you are, Lord," I thought, "in all your majestic glory!"

His closeness was totally comforting.

--

As we neared the Chicago airport, I began to get a bit nervous. Out the window, I saw the city and rows of houses on the ground. A deep feeling of dread came over me, which disturbed me, since I usually wanted to kiss the ground when I came home to the States. For the first time, I really didn't feel like being here. A little cloud of anxiety and stress started to settle on me.

Someone from TEAM had made arrangements for us to avoid the news reporters when our plane docked at the airport. Four people met us at the gate and took us out a side door, where our bags were waiting. It was a relief not to have to see anyone from the press.

Soon, we were in a large van headed toward Carol Stream.[31] The people from our mission organization politely carried on an upbeat conversation. I nodded and shook my head, trying to participate so they'd know I was all right. Besides my dread, I had a feeling of extreme tiredness, since I hadn't slept much in the week since Herb was abducted. I hadn't eaten much either. Suddenly, it felt like I had reached the limit of human endurance—I thought I was going to fall apart right here, right here in the van.

31 At that time Carol Stream, Illinois, a suburb of Chicago, was the location of TEAM's headquarters.

"God, help me, please" I prayed. "I'm about to lose it!" My cloud of anxiety lifted quickly, and I felt renewed. I was still tired, but His peace was with me once again.

Christine and I were driven to the house of TEAM's director.[32] He and his wife were out of town, and they graciously offered to let us stay in their home.

One of the men who met us at the airport was Steve Edlin, the director of member care for our organization. He was a quiet person with a tranquil demeanor, always seeming to choose his words carefully.

"Are you okay to stay here by yourselves?" he asked. "Or would you like to have someone stay with you?"

Christine and I both wanted to stay by ourselves. They had stocked the house with food, helped us get our luggage upstairs, and did everything possible to make us feel at home and comfortable.

Once certain we'd be fine, Steve said, "Well, then, you two have a good night. I'll come around ten o'clock tomorrow morning for a time of debriefing."

"Oh, okay," I said, and waved as they left.

The next morning, Steve arrived and politely queried us about everything that had happened and how it made us feel. We sat in the family room, in a big comfortable couch, just the two of us with Steve, talking all morning. I didn't mind sharing what happened, but the "how it made me feel" part was a little unsettling. I hadn't really analyzed how the shock of Herb's kidnapping was making me feel.

Steve showed us a chart of how a traumatic event might be processed on a psychological basis: Initial reactions start with disorienting anxiety and a sense of numbness, and then follows a u-shaped curve down and back up before ending with having adjusted to the incident, coped, and returned to normal life. I recognized the initial reaction, but after the experience on the airplane, I felt that

---

32 George W. Murray served as the Executive Director of TEAM in the late 1990s. In 2000 he became the President of Columbia International University and later Chancellor of CIU, located in Columbia, South Carolina.

the Lord fast-forwarded me around the downward curve and back up a long way on the ascending curve. God had already healed my heart from much of the anxiety, though trying times still lay ahead.

"There's something I need to tell you," I said cautiously. "I feel it is important you should know, in order to understand my debriefing better."

"That's fine, Linda," he said. His tone of speech was calm.

Steve listened attentively while I described my encounter with God. I couldn't tell by his reaction what he was thinking, but I felt somewhat awkward telling the story.

The TEAM mission brought lunch to the house, and several people came by to eat during our stay. Everyone was helpful and caring, and there was always lots of food.

Christine called her parents and learned that her close friend's father had passed away, so she made plans to fly home to Boston within a couple of days. I decided to call Amy and ask if she would fly out to Chicago and then fly home with me after the full debriefing. She said she'd come right away.

I was excited, because for a long time I had been hoping she could meet Christine, who had become like a daughter to me. She and Amy had a lot of common interests, and both were outgoing, with beautiful singing voices. I was certain they would love each other. They did, as soon as they met.

On the ride home from the Chicago airport, Christine and Amy started reminiscing about Herb and the funny way he said or did things.

"I love the way he rubs his nose when he's speaking and gets nervous," Amy said.

"Oh, I know," Christine agreed, nodding. "And how he always says he's serious about not eating junk food or drinking Coke except for his 'day off,' when he eats more junk and drinks more Coke than he would if he'd been munching every day."

Amy laughed. "Or when he sits down to pray and starts snoring, but when you ask what he was doing, he says he was praying, of course, even though we all heard him snoring!"

The three of us were laughing hysterically. The reminiscing helped break so much recent tension and it was refreshing to talk about the things that endeared Herb to us. Steve was quiet during the drive, since he really didn't know Herb or any of us, and I wondered if he thought we were all nuts.

We had a full day with Christine before she flew home. Amy and Christine sang for me; their voices blended beautifully. Such a special time, it was hard to say goodbye to Christine. She had been a wonderful gift from the Lord during our time in Russia and Dagestan and over the hectic days following Herb's abduction. I knew I would miss her. I gave her a long hug, and we promised to stay connected.

--

Steve asked me if I wanted to go to the chapel service at TEAM's headquarters.

"The home staff is praying fervently for Herb and for you," he said. "It would be an encouragement for them to see you."

"If I go, I'd like to share with them."

"I don't know . . ." Steve said. He was hesitant. "I think it might be too much stress for you to have to get up before so many people."

"But if they see me and don't know how good God has been to me," I reasoned, "it would be like withholding His glorious presence from them."

What I realized was that I hadn't been given my encounter experience just for myself, but to edify others. I really needed to be faithful and explain to others at the chapel service how God had so magnificently revealed Himself to me.

Amy and I went to the chapel service in the morning. People packed the room.. It was good to see everyone, including some old friends. They hugged me and told me how much they loved me.

I could see how concerned everyone was and how much love and compassion they had for Herb.

The time of worship had a song I'd never heard before that spoke of seeing the glory of the Lord. It touched my heart and gave me courage, since I *had* seen the glory of the Lord. Amy then got up and sang "Sacred Delight," a song I love. As she sang, I felt like crying, but instead I tried to focus carefully on the words.

When it was my turn, I stood up at the front and explained what happened in Makhachkala, in Moscow, and on the airplane ride to Chicago. I urged everyone, if they had friends who didn't believe that God was real, to share my experiences or to send them to me.

"God didn't give this encounter to me just or myself," I said, "but for others—that they might have assurance in His grace. God will be protecting Herb. He is at work for good in all of these happenings." I hoped everyone there would be forever encouraged by knowing how absolutely magnificent is our God!

--

Amy and I landed back home in Arizona on Wednesday, November 25, on a cool and clear day. Her husband Steve and little Caleb were waiting for us at the airport – it was a special blessing to see them again.

We arrived the day before Thanksgiving. For the holiday dinner, our family ate with Herb's parents, Herb's sister and her family. My heart was full, and I wanted desperately to say something, though I didn't want to speak unless somebody asked me to.

Everyone gathered around the table, which was brimming with food and delicious scents. I just finished praying silently that God would have someone ask me to speak if He wanted me to say something, when my brother-in-law asked me if I had anything to say before we began.[33]

---

33 The family Thanksgiving gathering, and dinner took place in Phoenix at the home of Herb's sister, Patricia Weikart. Her husband Bill asked Linda to say something. Other family members present included Herb's mother and father, Virginia and Herb Gregg, Sr., daughter Amy Gregg Glover, her husband Steve and their son Caleb, and son Jason Gregg and his fiancé Linda Trower.

I nodded, and thanked him.

"Because we have been overseas so much," I told Herb's family, "I don't think you know what a great person the Lord has developed Herb into."

I spoke from my heart and quoted Jim Elliot: "He is no fool who gives what he cannot keep to gaining what he cannot lose."[34]

"Herb is a special person," I said. "He has labored for things eternal that cannot be lost, sometimes at the expense of material things that cannot be kept. What's happened is not a mistake. Herb is in the right place. We just have to pray and trust God."

I then asked Jason, our son, to pray. He prayed that the Lord would keep Herb safe and provide food for him to eat, and he thanked God for His love for us and for the meal.

Herb's father cried throughout dinner and couldn't eat.

--

Slowly, I fell back into daily life. The days seemed to pass somehow. God now helped me make it through the ordinary days, one day at a time.

A few weeks after I returned home, we received a copy of a video from Herb's captors. It had been delivered to the Russian government, on to the American government and our mission group, and then finally forwarded to us.

Amy and I put it in the tape player and sat down to watch it together. The tape flicked on to an image of Herb, who was sitting on the ground, handcuffed to a pipe. I stifled a gasp. I thought Herb looked terrible, with sores and marks on his face, like he'd been beaten.

In Russian, Herb said he wasn't well, he was cold and sick, and that the captors who had him were serious, that we needed to

---

34 Philip James Elliot (1927-1956) was a well-known Christian missionary and martyr who was sharing God's Word with the Huaorani peoples living in Ecuador. Unexpectedly, they murdered him and four of his colleagues. Elliot's wife Elisabeth later wrote two inspirational books about Elliot's life and missionary work, titled *Through Gates of Splendor* (1981) and *Shadows of the Almighty* (1989).

come up with three and a half million dollars! I was scared. It was frightening to see Herb locked up in some strange place, obviously being abused. The experience was shocking for both Amy and me, but we made it through the short video.

Right after the video ended, Jason arrived home and wanted to see it. We played the tape again. Jason watched it closely, examining the picture.

"I don't think dad looks that bad," he said when the tape ended.

"What?"

"No, he doesn't." Jason pointed to the TV screen saying, "When they told him to take off his cap, he did it immediately—so he's still physically strong. He's scared, but he's just repeating what they told him to say. And I bet the handcuffs were only for effect."

The three of us watched the video again, and to my amazement we now could see what was being presented in a more encouraging light. Herb indeed looked nervous, but he did not seem to be as bad off as I first thought. At least we could see that he was alive – what a relief that was! Watching the video was upsetting, especially in picturing Herb being held captive so far away. But as we prayed for him, we had hope.

Christmas quickly came along. I found it a bit hard to get ready for the holidays without Herb, but a friend loaned us their cabin so we could get away as a family, a wonderful blessing. We bought a couple gifts for each other, and bought one for Herb, too. His gift was a large painting of a river with beautiful trees, a peaceful scene for him to look at once released from captivity.

The painting sat up in a corner, waiting for him to open it.

Our little grandson Caleb helped us have joy. This was his second Christmas, and he was delighted with everything. The rest of us laughed at his happy antics, even as we contemplated in another part of our brains what kind of Christmas Herb would be experiencing somewhere in Chechnya.

VIII

KICKING

Herb

Into the New Year, the Outpost

Thanksgiving came and went, as did Christmas, various birthdays and anniversaries. Many days and important dates skidded by me in the washroom. I noted them as they occurred, though there was not much to do. It was a bad feeling, but God wanted me to thank Him as these dates passed, rather than feel sorry for myself.

After the New Year, things became heavier at the outpost. One night, around the first of January, Cap tried to convince me of the truth of jihad Islam. It was a very intense and satanic barrage.

I was sitting on an old mat up in the third floor classroom where we made our videos and ransom calls. Cap brought me up just for this talk. We were alone in the large, quiet classroom. For the first time, Cap's face was not covered by a terrorist head mask, but the room was left unusually dark, so I couldn't see him that clearly. I concentrated instead on his words and how to respond properly.

Cap was on a real fanatical level from the start, and it escalated throughout the conversation. His purpose, it seemed, was to browbeat me into accepting their faith. He got right in front of me and started bombarding me with various Islamic doctrines.

"God is one!" he said.

I nodded – I agreed with him whenever possible.

"Jesus was not a Jew," he spat, angrily. "His death and resurrection was a big lie. He was not even on the cross—it was another disciple, someone who looked like him."

I didn't respond to this comment, and Cap could tell I didn't agree. It was very clear that the idea of Christ being God was anathema to Cap. The jihadis believed that Jesus was a holy man, but that the greatest of all the prophets was Mohammad. Cap talked about the Pentateuch and how it prophesied a great leader like Moses, but in his mind the words referred to Mohammad.

"You do not know anything about Islam," Cap said, frustrated with me.

"No, I don't know much," I admitted. I tried to be calm and reasonable in response to Cap's aggression. I even consented to read their holy book, the Koran, if Cap could get a copy for me in English.

Cap worked his way through a number of their beliefs, growing more ardent with each one. He could see I was agreeable about many points, but just wouldn't agree on the most crucial issue: Jesus. I was not swallowing his doctrines, and it irked him.

"That's enough," he finally declared. "Let's go back to your room."

He led me back to the washroom, and I was relieved the session was over. But relations changed after that night. As a result of our conversation, Cap told his buddies to harass me. From then on, the kicking started, though they rarely kicked me hard. The whole program was to intimidate me and break me down.

I discovered that these guys had two ways of talking: one way was to intimidate, with a rough and threatening voice, and the other was to act normal, with kindness and calmness. The intimidating style now became the norm, as well as the kicks. When they served me the food (stale white bread and boiled macaroni), they would often punish me with a kick.

Some jihadis liked to kick me more often than others. Kicker (I made up names since I didn't know my captors' actual names) definitely welcomed every opportunity to give me a nasty kick.

There was another guy I called "K.A." standing for "Kicker Alpha." He spoke in a country way and was very athletic. K.A. was sporadically a substitute food server who started out being very ugly with me. He enjoyed kicking too, though not quite as much as Kicker.

There were two old coats that I used as covers when sleeping. They had been in the room when I arrived and were obviously for use as bedding. Oddly, both coats had a Russian woman's name written on their labels, likely the names of previous captives. I learned to throw one of the coats over me when someone came into my room, so that it covered my neck, shoulders, back, and side. This blunted the sharpness of the kicks. Amazingly, the jihadis didn't make me take the coat off, probably because the violence was mostly for show. A few times, they got the side of my head; more frequently, they hit my ribs.

The jihadis were really good at karate, and they could kick with pinpoint accuracy. One guy kicked my face once, but his foot barely touched the end of my nose.

The abuse was clearly part of a conscious change in my kidnappers' strategy. One day, as part of their psych-out system, three jihadis came into my room acting tough.

"We want you to clean these sinks and make everything spic and span," they said. "If you don't, something serious will happen."

It was totally unreasonable. They gave me nothing to clean with, so I just did it by hand and used a lot of elbow grease. When the jihadis came back and saw that I had cleaned the sinks, they didn't say anything and dropped the subject.

A couple of the guys liked to barge in and ask, "Are you going to accept Islam?" When I replied in the negative, they would kick me again.

It was always a daunting question, because I knew a kick would come if I said no. I felt really shaken. Many times it would take me awhile to regain my composure after they left the room. I'd sit quietly under my coat, waiting for my emotions to calm down and for the peace of God to refill my mind and body.

Often, I would answer, "I already believe in Allah," and as the conversation went on, say, "God is one." I was trying to show them that we all believed in God. Because many of the jihadis did not really understand spiritual matters, most of them accepted my answer, which somewhat eased the situation.

As time went along, different jihadis would come into my room to ask various questions. I was an anomaly: an American and a Christian. These guys had their system for brow-beating people, but I was a new kind of person, and many were curious.

One time, the driver from the jeep came in to visit me. At first, I thought he was going to be violent, but I was pleased to find that he was only coming in to chat and get to know me better. We had a long, friendly talk. He tried to cheer me up, joking about putting up a basketball hoop in the washroom. He also talked about America.

"*America bardok*," he said—"America's a mess."

The driver was referring to all the confusion caused by freedom of choice and religious liberty, the rampant immorality and all turmoil that was so prevalent. He was surprised that I agreed with him. My admission helped bond us. He was not as fanatical as some of the other jihadis. His father had been killed in the recent war with Russia, and he was simply continuing with the Chechen cause of seeking full independence from the Soviets.[35]

Another time, two jihadis broke the lock on my door to get into my room. I didn't know what they wanted, so I was on my face

35 Casualties in the First Chechen War (1994-1996), fought over the desire of Chechnya to gain complete independence from Russia, were brutally high. See the estimated causality numbers presented in the foreword,. This war gained the Chechen rebels a few years of independence, but the Second Chechen War (1999-2009) forced this defiant nation back into the Russian fold.

before God, pleading for help. As matters turned out, they were coming in to deliver me food; apparently, the food server was gone, and they didn't have a key.

One of the young men was very inquisitive. He asked what life was like in America. He asked if I'd read the Koran and why I didn't bow down to Allah five times a day at the set times.

"I always talk to God," I explained. "I don't have to bow down. I can bow or pray in any other position. But there are no set prayer times—all the time is prayer time."

This young fellow listened politely. He didn't cover his face, and I noticed he was very good looking, like a movie star: grizzled, but not bearded, with a western haircut that was not the typical Chechen look. He seemed positive and nice, although there was a big shiny hunting knife strapped to his belt. He and the other guy stayed for several minutes, asking me questions.

Many of the jihadis developed a respect for me as we talked, even as they learned more about me. As a result two factions emerged in the outpost. One group, which I called the "Hawks," hated me with a passion and wanted me dead immediately. They would talk about me in their rooms, about how they wanted to cut off my hand and kill me. The other group, the "Doves," wanted to keep me alive in order to get the ransom money.

--

In the middle of January, around the 16th, we made our second videotape. Cap came in, grabbed my shoulder and hustled me up to the classroom. He was so agitated that his breathing was labored. It made me nervous. As I consciously tried to stay calm, following his commands and responding to his questions, he also seemed to calm down.

Cap operated the camcorder, and Hassan assisted him. Because my Russian was so poor, Cap decided to let me make my statement in English. Once again, he told me exactly what to say: I was supposed to convey that my situation was much worse than before and that my health was really bad. He wanted me to say my missionary sponsors should help me because they and organizations like them helped people all over the world, and here I was in desperate straits, so they should assist one of their own.

I also had to instruct them to come up with $3.5 million within one month. If the jihadis didn't receive the money by that time, a hand or foot would be cut off, and my ransom would be raised to $4 million. Cap had me advise TEAM and Linda about possible different ways to raise the money—or else.

With this cassette, the same pickup arrangement would be used as before, first stashed in the electrical box then carried by Timur to Russian officials in Moscow.

After the recording, Hassan showed me a page from an Islamic newspaper that had an article about four technicians who were recently killed at the killing camp. Three of the victims were British and the fourth was from New Zealand. They had been decapitated, and the paper showed four little square pictures of their heads. Cap told me that the price set for their release and survival was $5.5 million, but the *mujahadeen*, the holy warriors who held them, despised the ransom idea and so cut off their heads.[36]

Hassan waved the paper in front of me. "This is your future if you don't come up with the money," he said.

Cap nodded, smirking. Their tone of voice and demeanor was totally heartless and hateful. They did not cover their faces with their head coverings, which gave me a very fearful feeling. They weren't worried about my seeing what they actually looked like—all of which seemed to suggest that I wasn't going to survive much longer.

---

36 These merciless killings gained international attention and smeared the reputation of Chechnya as a safe place for well capitalized foreign interests to invest or conduct business. The victims' heads were found in early December along a road near Grozny; the bodies were recovered in the same area toward the end of that month. It's possible that these victims were held in a killing camp somewhere outside Grozny. For more information, see Chapter 10, footnote 40, in a passage where State Department official Bill Daniels shares the same gruesome information with Linda.

I had to work at not letting my heart sink. Since neither Cap nor Hassan showed concern about not wearing their head covers, I tried to act normal while looking at their faces and answering their questions.

However, it was the first time I got a look at Cap and Hassan. Hassan was like a high school football player: athletic, muscular, clean shaven. He was younger, in his twenties with light skin and dark hair. Cap was a bit older. He was average in height, a little bit chubby and not as athletic looking like Hassan. He had a medium length beard with moustache and sideburns, all black – he had very dark coloring.

Cap was pure Chechen. My immediate impression of his face was his cruel expression: His eyes were squinted shut, like slits of malice in a kind of mocking bravado. But I sensed that his boisterous actions were mostly a game.

Cap and Hassan acted as though the $3.5 million ransom was completely reasonable and accessible to my organization. Hassan tried to make me admit that it was not too much to demand.

He pointedly asked me, "That's not too much, is it?"

"That's a lot," I said.

Hassan began making threats about the killing camp, trying to intimidate me into getting the money.

"You will go to the camp in a month, and you will die," he almost shouted. Hassan, more than Cap, appeared to enjoy this thought. He seethed hostility.

"It's terrible there," he continued. "The food is terrible, like trash—the type of trash that dogs scrounge up."

Cap reached over and felt my chest and stomach, patting up and down, and acted surprised to find any substance there. I had not yet lost very much weight from the meager diet, and he was making light of it.

"You will really thin down while waiting for the money to come," he joked. He had a bizarre sense of humor. "If you go to the camp, you will surely lose a lot of weight."

For the time being, Cap said, I would not be going to the camp. He had high hopes that the money would arrive soon.

--

Cap and Hassan then tried to talk me into believing in their jihadist version of Islam through a fear approach. I didn't say anything in response to their browbeating, but sat passively and listened to their commentary.

Both of them affirmed that I was going to hell.

"You should not consider yourself a good person, worthy of heaven," Cap said. "The only way to heaven is by following the Koran."

He gave half a dozen examples of activities the Koran pointed out as being necessary for salvation, such as using your money well and giving to the poor. Some of the requirements struck me as ridiculous, and ironic, considering the activities that went on at the outpost.

On many occasions, Cap explained their doctrinal ideas, sometimes with Hassan and sometimes alone. Cap never asked me, "Are you going to accept Islam?" like the kicking jihadis; he tried to be more psychological. We would usually be doing something else, like working up in the classroom, and he'd start talking. Other times, he'd come into my room to talk. As the weeks passed, he gave me more chances to respond, and I was forced to play the learner part.

The jihadis believed the Koran was sublime, detailing how we should live in all aspects of life. I was somewhat amazed how Cap would describe the Koran with rapt contentment, saying how wonderful it was, hoping to convince me. He was pleased when I agreed to read it, though he could never find a copy in English, and he knew I couldn't read well enough in Russian.

He affirmed that all the ancient people of the world were giants. Their evil was monstrous, as well as their size, and the creator made them gigantic so they would have more body surface in hell for punishments. The reason modern man was much smaller, he claimed, was to curtail sin.

"Imagine if people today were that huge," Cap said to me. "With all their sinfulness, how much more evil would exist in the world!"

Only a few things were eternal, they believed. One of them was fire; they seemed to connect fire to God. Another eternal object was a microscopic seed in the tailbone. In the current age, people came into the world through birth, but in the next age, this seed would be planted in the ground and people would sprout up.

Cap also told me that it was important for a man to have a beard: it helped his brain function better. He pointed out how many men of God in the past wore beards. While Cap and some of the other jihadis related a number of these more fanciful ideas to me, I worked hard to maintain a straight face, knowing that my seeming acceptance of such beliefs was important for my survival.

One discussion with Cap gave me a lot of insight into his reason for being a jihadi. He described how a certain type of person thought he would have eternal life but would fail in the righteous judgment of God. Another type would believe he was saved but was not. He listed different types of people—the rich, those who went to the mosque all the time, this type of person, that type of person, and so on—all thinking self-confidently, but unable to escape God's punishment. What Cap showed was his feeling about how difficult it was to gain entrance into the kingdom of God. I could see why he and the jihadis were battling so intensely to avoid hell and gain paradise.

Fear of God was an important principle for the jihadis. Once, I mentioned being afraid of the killing camp. Cap replied, "Don't fear man—fear God." This was a common phrase. Even the driver, when he came to chat with me, first asked, "You fear God, don't you?" Fearing God was one of their standards of a good man. When they saw that I was a believer who also feared God, it helped in their treatment of me.

Through time, I came to understand that the outpost and its brand of Islam was based on hatred—and fed on their anger. The jihadis communicated their hatred for Russians and Russian Orthodoxy. They detested the processions and the cross associated with the Russian Orthodox Church.

K.A. asked me one night, in a very intense voice, if I had a cross. "No," I replied, thinking he must mean a necklace with a cross or something similar attached.

"It's good that you don't have one," he said. The loathing in his voice was powerful; it was the first time in my life when I could physically feel hate coming from a person.

I also found out that the jihadis really hated Jews. They despised them. They felt the Jews were behind much of what was wrong with the world, and they believed Jews controlled most of big business operations. They had the idea that there were a lot of Jews in the U.S., that Americans were close to them in friendship, and that America and Israel were in cahoots on everything. One of the guys at the outpost even said they would not rest until Jerusalem belonged to the Muslims. An important part of their jihad was to destroy the Jews.

Cap had asserted to me that the first chapter of the Koran was about jihad, a holy war. They believed this Scripture gave them justification to kill and cause suffering for anyone who disagreed with them. The Chechens hated most Dagestanis because the latter, as a whole, did not practice jihad. They considered the Dagestanis to be false, tainted, worldly Muslims—the same as they viewed all Muslims who did not embrace jihad.

For this reason, a lot of the kidnap victims in Chechnya came from Dagestan and other Russian Muslim republics nearby. In addition to obtaining ransom money, the jihadis wanted to make people convert. Cap and Hassan both affirmed to me that they had converted to this form of Islamic faith. In a moment of truth, Cap even told me that *he* too had been a captive! I was dumbfounded.

"You mean, before then you didn't believe?" I asked, shocked.

Cap would not say any more about this matter. He realized that he had let out too much personal information. We were alone when he told me this confession, and his guard was down because, at heart, he was a Dove. As we began spending more time together, Cap grew to like me, despite himself. Because of his allegiance to the jihadis, he really wanted me to convert to his religion. At least that was what I perceived at the time.

I came to realize that one of the profound differences between radical Islam and Christianity was the issue of love. I had known this already, but I experienced it in the flesh at the outpost.

In conversations, I would tell these young jihadis that Allah was love, that I believed in Allah, talked and prayed to Him constantly, and that He loved me. It surprised and appealed to many of them.

They were used to hearing that "God is one" or that "God is great," but they were not accustomed to hearing that "God is love." The jihadis didn't know how to respond; this thought seemed like something new to them. Eventually, all the jihadis at the outpost heard me say this in conversation or heard it from one of their associates. My constant prayer was the God's healing love would seep into their hearts and minds.

The jihadis had great respect for *Isa—they* used the Arabic name for Jesus, which softened their feelings somewhat. They knew Jesus lived a life of love.

Early on, I heard one of the jihadis blurt out, "I love Isa." His colleagues said nothing in reply. These were young, religiously motivated soldiers, and theology was often on their minds. They hadn't been exposed to much doctrine beyond the tenets of jihad. Their radical faith was a source of their anger toward those who did not agree with their ways of both perceiving and worshipping Allah.

I couldn't always be direct in talking about God's love, so I tried to convey this message through my attitude and actions. The weeks kept rolling along. The kicking became sporadic, but not so with various intimidating games, especially when the Hawks would talk about chopping off my hand. Thanks be to God and His love that helped me stay calm and at peace while enduring my captivity at the outpost each and every day.

IX

INTROSPECTION

Herb

January-February 1999, the Outpost

Now there would be long stretches of time—usually three or four days but sometimes as many as seven days—when I would have no contact beside the food server. The solitary confinement did not bother me; all the hours sitting or lying in my room were very conducive to meditative thinking. I could review Bible passages, pray for people freely, and reminisce about my life.

As I thought about my past years, I realized that God had stopped me cold in my tracks. Never before in my Christian walk had I taken time to reflect upon my life and service before the Lord in an extended time, never in thirty-three years! I was always too caught up in the activities and challenges of the present. For the first time, I began to reminisce about my life, both before and after becoming a Christian.

In this reflection, the Holy Spirit began convicting me. Day after day and week after week, the Lord, the holy God, revealed sins and sin patterns in me. I saw that He was pruning me, which in itself encouraged me about surviving. I figured He was doing this for me to bear fruit in the future and not for me to be killed somewhere in Chechnya. I remembered what He said in John 15:2 about bearing fruit: *Every branch in Me that does not bear fruit, He takes away; and every branch that bears fruit, He prunes it so that it may bear more fruit.*

I was moved to confess and repent of one sin after another. He even showed me sins I did not realize were there: sins like pride—it was humbling to be forced to get on all fours when the kidnappers came into my room—and also lack of love, lack of faith, lack of kindness and consideration, lack of prayer, not always rejoicing, not asking the Lord for wisdom, not being careful with my words, and allowing bad attitudes to squelch the fruit of the Spirit. I was convicted of always being so rushed that I allowed busy-ness to squeeze out vital time for prayer and meditation.

The Lord helped me repent of these sins. Right there, in my washroom, the Lord began giving me victory. What a God of victory! I finally understood why I had lacked so much joy in my spiritual pilgrimage: those sin patterns had been binding me and limiting my joy. Now peace and joy came to me in floods.

I realized that God was performing some wonderful acts in my plight. In the process of revealing and convicting me of sin, He was reviving me. He actually gave me a personal "revival" in the dark little washroom! Because of this cleansing, the Lord was more able to reflect something of Christ through my life to the poor, deceived jihadi young men in the outpost.

He was also giving me the privilege of suffering for Him and His Name's sake. I knew this was one of the reasons the Lord allowed me to be kidnapped. Philippians 1:29 said, *For to you it has been granted for Christ's sake, not only to believe in him, but also to suffer for his sake.* Other verses spoke to me, as well, including Philippians 3:10-11, Romans 8:16-17, and II Timothy 2:3, which said, *Suffer hardship for me, as a good soldier of Christ Jesus.*[37]

---

37 **Philippians 3:10-11**: I want to know Christ—yes, to know the power of his resurrection and participation in his sufferings, becoming like him in his death, and so, somehow, attaining to the resurrection of the dead. **Romans 8:16-17**: The Spirit himself testifies with our spirit that we are God's children. Now if we are children, then we are heirs—heirs of God and co-heirs with Christ, if indeed we share in his sufferings in order that we may also share in his glory.

To stay spiritually fit, I developed daily spiritual routines in my solitude. Concerning meditation: I tried to meditate on His Word day and night, as Psalm 1:2-3 and Joshua 1:8 say to do.[38] I would put passages in pictures in my mind and think of other verses that related in cross references. I would ponder over both Old Testament and New Testament portions.

Reviewing Bible chapters or parts of chapters helped me to control my mind and attitudes. I would go over Psalms 19 and 23, and the first part of Psalm 46: *God is our refuge and strength, a very present help in trouble.* Also, I would think about Matthew 5:1-16, the parables of Matthew 13, John 15:1-11, and the first chapter of Ephesians.

Memorizing Scripture had been imperative to me since my conversion. Even in my first year of faith, I knew something about the importance of the Word and the necessity of having it in my mind and heart in a permanent way. I began with the Navigators' Topical Memory System, memorizing a couple verses each week, which I did for years.. Then, I started memorizing Bible chapters. One of my favorite verses was Matthew 4:4: *Jesus answered, "It is written: 'Man does not live on bread alone, but on every word that comes from the mouth of God.'"* Another was Matthew 6:33: *But seek first his kingdom and his righteousness, and all these things will be given to you as well.*

The names of God I could remember from Scripture really encouraged me at the outpost: "Elohim" reminded me that the Lord was omnipotent; "Yahweh" reminded me that He was the covenant-keeping, warring God of Israel; "Adonai" reminded me that He was the owner of everyone and everything; and "Jehovah Jireh" reminded me of His ability to see and provide for our needs.

38 **Psalms 1:2-3**: But whose delight is in the law of the LORD, and who meditates on his law day and night. That person is like a tree planted by streams of water, which yields its fruit in season and whose leaf does not wither—whatever they do prospers. **Joshua 1:8**: Keep this Book of the Law always on your lips; meditate on it day and night, so that you may be careful to do everything written in it. Then you will be prosperous and successful.

God provided for me each day. He gave me everything that I needed, down to the smallest, most mundane details. When my book that I used for toilet tissue was running low, I asked Nice for another old book or newspaper. He asked me why and I told him. Nice was scandalized; he was an old-fashioned fellow who thought I should use water like they did in seventh-century Arabia. A week or so went by and I asked him again, but he never brought me any paper. I was down to my last few squares of paper. Within days, however, my food server changed to "Ping"—Ping gave me another old book.

Ping was a top-notch ping pong player. He became my food server in February, and he was with me for a pretty long stretch of time. When he delivered my food, he often stayed to chat, and I'd try to ask him questions to be friendly.

Ping and I interacted quite a bit, and we got to know each other over time. We'd talk about our lives, and I asked him where he was born, whether or not he was from a village, and what his life was like. He told me that he came from a Russian Orthodox background but converted to Islam. Ping was pure Chechen, though his eyes and some of his features looked Chinese. His attitude was always kind and thoughtful—unusually so for a jihadi.

I heard helicopters overhead frequently. A bunch would fly past in the morning, and they would return in the evening. Ping let it slip one day that there was a Chechen base nearby, and I thought the outpost must be close to an airport. I assumed we were near the border of Chechnya and Dagestan, but I didn't know what side we were on. In fact, it was very difficult for me to guess where we were.

--

In the last week of February, an English-speaking couple with a British accent arrived at the outpost. They appeared to be friends and co-workers of the jihadis, quite accepted and trusted. When they came, the militants were happy to see them.

"Debbie!" one of the jihadis exclaimed.

The man's name was Peter. They seemed to be suppliers of medicine, food, or some other objects. They had a very cordial relationship with these paramilitaries, and they spent about a week at the outpost before their planned departure. I could hear them use English with one another and with Philip. They spoke Russian, with some Portuguese words and phrases, to the jihadis.

Cap had Peter and Debbie watch my January video, supposedly to corroborate that what I said was what I was supposed to say. During the filming, I'd had a strong urge to wink once while the camcorder worked, but instead decided to play it straight and convincingly as they wanted. I was glad I hadn't done that: Peter or Debbie would have spotted and understood that wink.

--

Shortly after Peter and Debbie arrived, I heard a struggle on the floor above me. Previously, for many nights, I had heard Bear haranguing a youth who likely was nabbed from Dagestan. They would hold interrogation sessions in the third-floor classrooms almost directly above my room. Bear would harass and intimidate this guy night after night. Sometimes, I heard loud thumps on the floor, and I came to understand that Bear was throwing the young man around. As he landed on the floor, I would hear the thud. Such a noise was unnerving.

The victim was probably a teen, totally uncooperative. He did not want to believe their doctrines, nor supply Bear and his buddies with information that would help the kidnappers weasel money out of his relatives. After hearing the threats and thumping for many nights, I listened to the struggle.

One of the jihadis yelled, "*Eta nyelzyá!*"—"It is prohibited!"

The teen had tried to escape, and they had grabbed him.

The next morning, they brought this youth downstairs in order to haul him off to the city jail—often the police worked with the jihadis. This victim was flailing like a caught fish, kicking desks and fighting against his captors, but he was outnumbered and outmuscled. The scuffle started upstairs, but the sounds of the struggle descended as the jihadis forced him downstairs. They eventually dragged him outside.

Later, in the middle of the night, I heard someone say, "*Ya yevó ubeél*"—"I killed him."

The voice was directed to Bear, who had been waiting in a room near mine.

"*Da?*" Bear said casually—"Yeah?"

Bear walked to another room to sleep. His footsteps stomped heavily on the floor, moving down the hall in the quiet outpost.

I felt numb knowing that Bear and the other Hawks could take my life as easily at any time. Thank God that He was there each and every day for me as I offered my prayers and introspective thoughts with Him.

X

Perseverance

Linda

January-February 1999

Much more happened in Russia than I knew—not all of the details were passed along to me. Herb's captors tried to get a hold of me several times, but we were instructed not to answer their calls. Once, Amy picked up the phone, not thinking, and then immediately hung up when she realized who was calling. To help screen calls, we added an answering machine. The machine recorded Herb in one of their calls, and I secretly listened to it every day: his voice saying, "Hello? Hello?"

The team in Moscow was under a lot of stress. They were putting in a tremendous amount of time and effort, trying to help with negotiations. Phil Cantrell, our team leader there, went to the embassy frequently, both getting news and encouraging Counsel General Laura Clerici and other officials there to do whatever possible to get Herb freed safely.

The team had little contact with the Russian Internal Affairs Police who were the official investigators and the ones responsible to work for Herb's release, or with Mr. K, their negotiator. Still, they worked diligently, being TEAM's representatives in the country. We were not able to have much contact with each other, except for one time when all the team members there sent me an audio tape with messages from each of them, saying how much they cared—a truly kind gesture—and how they were continually praying for Herb's liberation.

I was able to contact our Dagestani church group only once. It was when Christine and I were in Chicago after first arriving in the States from Russia. They were worried about how we were doing, but they felt encouraged to hear us sounding normal. We told them that we would keep praying for them.

Shortly after the New Year, our mission assigned a man named John Jackson to be my liaison with our organization's home office. He was the head of TEAM's communication department, and he was perfect for the job. John called me nearly every day with any news—good or bad—and often he would simply call to see how I was doing. My family just fell in love with John. We all greatly appreciated his calls.

Sometimes, John would fly out to visit us in person, coming to check on us and to be supportive. He was always positive and encouraging, buoying up any unhappy news with Scripture. To take such responsibility was a great personal strain for John. We realized that constantly attending to us was a time sacrifice for John and his family, and we loved him all the more for it.

--

The U.S. State Department also gave me a liaison: Bill Daniels.[39] Bill was of a different sort. He was a funny man, experienced in his work, and very direct. One of my first calls from Bill came in December.

"Hi, Linda," he said, "it's Bill."

"Hello, Bill. How are you?"

"I'm fine. I have some good news for you."

"Really?" I was excited. "What is it?"

"Well, there were four foreigners who were beheaded in

39 Daniels worked in the State Department's Bureau of Consular Affairs' Office of Overseas Citizen Services.

Chechnya," Bill explained. "I'm sure it will be on the news, but I wanted you to know first that Herb's head was not one of them."

"Oh . . . okay."

The men were technicians who had been abducted in October. Their company was negotiating with the captors toward a price for their release, but then the heads unexpectedly were found on a road outside of Grozny. It was unclear what went wrong, but Bill said the State Department thought it was a botched rescue attempt on the part of the Russians. Sometime later, a news investigation suggested that foreign terrorists working with al-Qaeda and Osama bin Laden paid the captors millions of dollars to kill the technicians instead.[40]

Bill called me every month, usually saying, "I just got back from Syria . . ." or some other place. Herb wasn't the only case that Bill was handling, and since he wasn't based in Moscow, he was sometimes frustrated by what the embassy or the Russians wouldn't say. But Bill knew more than I did, and I liked it when he called because he was honest and not patronizing.

Since he had so much experience, Bill knew the reality of our situation, how remote Herb's chances of survival actually were, and what the odds were to save him. He had seen a lot of cases where matters didn't turn out well.

"There's really not much chance for him," Bill said, "but we can hope."

"My hope is in the Lord," I replied.

Bill chuckled. "You'll need it because there's only about a one percent chance they'll let him go."

---

40 These four victims were engineers working for the Granger Telecom Company, a British firm operating under contract to install a cellular phone system in the Chechen capital city of Grozny. Kidnapped on October 3, their heads were found two months later near a road in a forest outside of Grozny. Questions remain as to why they were abducted and killed. Some believe that Osama bin Laden allegedly paid the Arbi Barayev gang $30 million for the killings, supposedly because he wanted to rid Chechnya of foreign infidels. Herb's captors shared the same gruesome story with Herb (see Chapter 8, footnote 36) as a forewarning of what could happen to him if he didn't cooperate with Cap, Hassan, and his other captors in obtaining a large ransom payment.

"Well, why can't the American government just pay and get him out?" I asked.

"Oh, they never do that."

"If it were an ambassador, they'd use some weight."

"Oh, no, they wouldn't . . ."

Even though he was sometimes brusque, I appreciated Bill and his efforts. He always tried to keep government officials moving forward on the case and to keep Herb on their minds.

--

Toward the end of January, our whole family received an invitation to visit TEAM headquarters in Carol Stream, Illinois. Jason, Amy, her husband Steve, my grandson Caleb, and I all flew back to the Chicago area for the visit. The mission office staff showered their love on us, and we were able to have a delightful visit with John Jackson's family.

Our area director Dave Davis and the crisis adviser had flown in from Moscow. We had several meetings with them; we gained needed information to understand what exactly was going on with the negotiation process. They even provided a babysitter for Caleb so we could all attend everything. They told us a bit more about what was happening with the governments in Russia and explained the rationale behind their no-ransom policy. This was not a financial matter—on the contrary, TEAM spared no expense in working for Herb's release—but the policy was necessary to prevent other missionaries from being kidnapped.

Also, they told us that it wasn't wise to have much publicity about Herb's kidnapping. The captors might conclude that he was more important and valuable than they first realized, which might cause them to raise their ransom demand. My frustration almost boiled over, but I realized they were probably right.

However, TEAM did send prayer requests worldwide, and I steadily received letters and emails from men, women and lots of children who were praying for Herb's release. Amazingly for me, prayers swept across denominational boundaries and went out to the Lord from places all around the world. Many people said they would wake up at night with such a burden to pray for Herb. I began to consider that one of the reasons that the Lord allowed Herb to be kidnapped was to unify His people in prayer. It would be pleasing to God to answer positively all of these prayer requests.

--

When we returned to Arizona, I re-read a very old book called *Stepping Heavenward*.[41] In this novel, I came upon an experience of the woman in the story that challenged and comforted me: The woman explained how, through difficult challenges in her life, she must lie down on the river of God's will for her and let Him lead her wherever the current went. I pictured myself lying down on the river of God's will for me and floating calmly wherever He took me. Imagining lying down on that river brought me great peace.

Late in February, Steve, the counselor from our mission, came out for a visit. The difficult day had come when I needed to decide where to have Herb's body buried if he were killed. His brutal end was a possibility, we all knew, since the jihadis had beheaded those four men in December and killed many other hostages as well. I talked with my children, and we initially decided that if Herb were killed to bury his remains in Dagestan.

"Herb loved Dagestan," I told Steve, "and the people there loved him. Also, it would be nearby where he is now, so they wouldn't have to move him very far."

Steve thought for a moment, then said, "I'm not sure that's a good idea. You wouldn't be able to go to a funeral there or even visit the grave. Your family would not have closure."

I sighed, knowing that Herb wouldn't care where he was buried. While we were still in Dagestan, we had discussed what to do if one of us died, and we'd decided to just have the other one dig a

---

41 A novel originally published in 1869 and written by Elizabeth Payson Prentiss, *Heavenward* centers on a teenage girl facing life's challenges while maintaining her faith in God. Many modern editions still exist.

hole and bury us there. Such thoughts were not a big deal then, but now it seemed very important to decide.

"Well, where else could it be?" I wondered.

"What about Portugal?" Jason asked. "It's not as far away, and we could visit if we wanted."

We had worked in Portugal for 14 years, and we still had many friends there. There was a plot in a beautiful cemetery that our organization owned in Portugal—I agreed that we could take Herb's body there, if it came to that. This location would represent his heart to reach the unreached and have his remains placed in a beautiful country that our family loved.

Others didn't think this was a very good idea, but better than finding a location in Dagestan. I finally decided, if we had to have a funeral, to have it in Arizona with our friend Brent giving the message.[42] Brent would give a fiery challenge to reach the lost, a fervent message that Herb would want to be given at his funeral.

To balance out the task of choosing a burial site, Steve and I engaged in another, more positive and encouraging, task. We visited a counselor to see how I was doing and also to determine if I thought Herb would like this man should he need counseling when he regained his freedom. This thought was hopeful to me: the "when he got out" part.

I really did wonder if Herb would be emotionally stable after such a long time in captivity. The counselor was excellent. I liked him immediately, and I shared freely, even about the Lord revealing Himself to me on the plane. We had a rapport right away, and I knew Herb would also like him.

--

Throughout the winter, Herb's birthday came and went, along with Valentine's Day, my son-in-law Steve's birthday, Jason's birthday, and then Easter. Endless days rolled by as we waited, unable to influence

---

42 Brent Preston was a much respected TEAM colleague serving in Dagestan but happened to be back in the United States at the time of Herb's kidnapping.

anything. We kept hearing that his release would happen *soon*, but *soon* never seemed to come.

I knew God had a reason for Herb's kidnapping; I believed He was doing something with Herb wherever he was. But I wondered, as I washed dishes and changed the diapers of my fragile little grandson—the routine chores of life in America—I kept wondering what His purpose for me was, what He wanted me to do or learn during this time.

"God, I know you have Herb over there for a reason," I said, "but what do you want from me? What is all of this about for me?"

One day, while I was having my devotions in Romans, I came across these verses in Chapter Five that caught my attention: *And not only that, but we also glory in tribulations, knowing that tribulation produces perseverance; and perseverance, character; and character, hope.* I read these verses as if it was the first time. I was struck by the phrase "glory in tribulations."

"Can that be so?" I wondered. "How?"

Then I noticed the word "produces." Never before had I noticed that through tribulation God *produces* something.

"Oh, God," I said, "you're trying to *produce* something in me! But what?"

Re-reading the verses, I saw the word "perseverance." That was it: God was trying to produce perseverance in me, as each day of this trial rolled into another painful new day. It wasn't a short time in the fire before hopping out again, but months of staying in the fire, of hanging on through the uneventful days, when the normal things of life just didn't seem like they had always seemed before—and God was trying to teach me to persevere.

I thought about Jesus and the disciples in a boat on the Sea of Galilee when they were crossing the sea during a great storm. Jesus was asleep, the disciples were sure the boat was going to sink, and they started to freak out. They went to Jesus and yelled, "Wake up or we'll die!" Jesus woke up and then He calmed the storm.

"Oh, you of little faith," he said to the disciples.

Those words smacked me in the face: I was like the disciples, fearing the storm and wanting the bad weather to stop, but the Lord expected me to have faith.

"This is what you want from me, God," I realized, "to stay in the boat, not to freak out, and to trust that you will get us safely to the other side, despite the fierce wind and the waves."

I needed to stay in the boat and trust, but I knew God would have to help me, so I asked him please to help me to be calm and persevere, even though the storm kept on raging. Sometimes I actually pictured myself lying down beside Jesus in the boat as the storm raged on. I felt like there was some kind of heavenly spiritual battle taking place that would decide whether or not I would persevere and trust Jesus.

I also knew that it was important for my children to see me have faith—in many ways, waiting was harder for them because they hadn't had the vision I had experienced on the airplane. Knowing this gave me purpose and focus, and helped me understand what God had planned for those of us at home waiting for Herb.

Awhile after the Lord showed me these verses, I began to sense that things were getting tense with the negotiations for Herb. Something was wrong; it was already March, and he wasn't being released. I asked John Jackson and Bill Daniels what was going on, but they couldn't say what it was, only that there was a problem.

"Just stay in the boat," I reminded myself. "Stay in the boat and don't freak out . . . Lord, help me!"

I fought hard to persevere through the slow stretches of March and into April. The months felt so long, and Herb's release didn't happen and didn't happen. We believed Herb was still alive, but there was no news of him.

Then, early one morning, as I was out shopping at the grocery store, and my cell phone rang. The phone was just for me to receive updates about Herb, since our old phone line was never to be answered unless we recognized the number. John was generally the only person who called my cell phone, and it was unusually early for him to call.

"Hello," I said.

"Linda?"

"Yes."

"Hi, Linda. This is Steve."

I was surprised to hear Steve on the phone. Though he regularly called me from TEAM, to see how I was doing, he never called at 7:00 am like this.

"Hello, Steve. How are you?"

"I'm okay." He paused awkwardly. "I'm here in town."

Immediately, my mind flashed: "Herb is dead." I nearly fainted. My grip tightened on the grocery cart.

"Oh, no," I said. "Is something wrong?"

"Herb is still alive, but I have some news to tell you and the family. If you can get everyone together, I'll be right over."

I didn't know what to think. I left everything, abandoned my cart in the aisle, and rushed out of the store and back home.

XI

THE MARATHON BEGINS

Herb

February-March, the Outpost

On the afternoon of February 27, the British-type couple was leaving the outpost. They cordially said their goodbyes to the jihadis, and the last one they spoke to was Hassan. Their conversation went on and on. Apparently, they had developed a good friendship—not just because of Peter and Debbie's week at the outpost, but seemingly more long-standing. I strained to hear more through the walls of my washroom, but I couldn't make out their words.[43]

Finally, they concluded their conversation and were about to leave. I was desperate to stop Peter and Debbie, because I knew the outpost gang wanted to cut off my hand—the Hawks had been talking about doing so more often. I almost yelled out in English to try and convince them to take me with them. They were going to leave me alone with the Hawks. It was an awful feeling.

Hassan said goodbye to the couple, and as soon as they walked out, he rushed to some kind of kitchen not far from my room, to prepare to cut off my hand. Hassan had always been one of the most adamant Hawks. In the jihadi debates about what to do with me, I had heard him suggesting various ways to hurt me.

43 The nature of the business relationship involving Peter, Debbie, and the jihadis at the outpost remains unclear.

"I want to be the first in line to chop his hand off," Hassan said.

Now he began to follow through on his threats. He couldn't even wait until the couple had left the premises! It was amazing how strong his hatred was. He found some sort of flat board, probably for cutting meat. I could hear objects clanking and rattling as Hassan looked around for what he needed. He avidly gathered together items to perform his gruesome task while I fervently implored God for protection.

Somehow, Peter and Debbie heard about Hassan's actions, and they came back. I didn't dream they would stay, but they returned, and an intense argument took place. They dissuaded Hassan from his butchering plan, at least for the time being.

The next day, the same arguing occurred. Like guardian angels, Peter and Debbie decided to stay. They could see how bad matters were at the outpost, how I was in mortal danger. God miraculously worked in their hearts to stay on and fight for me. When Hassan again started preparing to chop off my hand, the couple again got in his face and managed to stop him.

Thus began what I called, the *Marathon Against Death*, an intense battle to mutilate or even terminate me. The money hadn't come. Everyone, even the men who first hauled me into their car, thought I would be out by February, and now the pressure was on. The Hawks wanted to cut off my hand and then transfer me to the killing camp; I called that place "Camp Awful."

The main method of killing men at the camp was the "*ócherud*," or "running through a gauntlet line"—a line of militants, each holding a club. Victims were forced to walk or run while getting repeatedly clubbed. The purpose was to bash in the person's head. I felt terrified to the point of numbness, not knowing how I could deal with such a death. I told God I would not be able to handle the gauntlet, and I believed He knew that.

On the third day of the intense conflict about my hand, Kicker was the one who wanted to cut it off. Again, the couple shielded me and talked the gang out of so brutal an action. They appealed to the jihadi's consciences, by saying things like, "his children will cry," and "he came out of love," and "he will die there." They appealed to the Doves who wanted the ransom money to keep me alive so as to receive the financial payload that was sure to come very soon.

Philip, the American guard at my door, joined Peter and Debbie in defending me. He was not a Dove when I first arrived at the outpost, and he had not said anything about me before this conflict erupted. Perhaps now he felt comfortable defending me because he was no longer alone—the couple was present, and they were very direct in confronting the Hawks.

Philip would talk with different soldiers outside my door, explaining where I was coming from as an American missionary and trying to persuade them to support me. Eventually, all the jihadis picked a side: Hawk or Dove.

For three weeks, the Hawks sought to chop off my hand and then have me transported to Camp Awful—I heard this every day for three full weeks. They especially wanted to cut off my hand before I went to the camp, in order to forward this gruesome specimen to the couriers in Makhachkala, who would carry the severed hand to the Russian and American officials in Moscow. The warning would be obvious—pay the ransom now or else something worse would soon happen.

Each morning, I heard the Hawks, usually led by Hassan, go down the hall from my room and begin gathering the instruments to cut me. The Doves would follow them, and long arguments ensued. The Hawks would finally back off for that day. As I listened to this jabbering, I thought how strange Hassan must have felt. It was like he was trapped in a big fishing net and unable to break through to do what he desperately wanted to do.

Though my captivity began in November, I now started reckoning time in terms of this "marathon" against my likely death. The Hawks were racing to kill me, and I was racing with God in hand to survive.

On the eighth day of the Marathon, the Hawks appeared to win the day in pushing to chop off my hand. In the afternoon, I listened to Hassan and his buddies as they decided to cut. I tried to prepare myself emotionally to walk out of my washroom and let them mutilate me. I debated with myself about whether or not to try and say something in my own defense, if they would even let me. A number of different options ran through my mind, various attempts to rationalize with the Hawks.

"Now wait a minute," I thought to argue, "let me say something . . ."

Or I might say, "How fair is this? How courageous is this?"

I also considered just showing my fear, having a nervous breakdown on the spot. But I didn't want to make them furious by what I said, knowing I would surely lose my life that way and not only my hand. So I decided to be quiet. Of course, I was horrified: but there was nothing to do but to deal with the situation calmly, praying all the time to God.

Two young Chechen jihadis opened the door of my room. They were short, bearded, and didn't cover their faces. I'd never seen them before. When they walked in, they didn't say anything. I was sitting, leaning against the wall, and stood up when they entered. One of the guys placed a hand on my shoulder and led me into the hallway. I went passively, expecting to lose my hand. It was an unbelievable feeling, walking down the hall—but the Lord gave me strength.

We went to another room, a space much larger than my little washroom. There was nothing in it except some grayish-green, close-cropped carpeting and a small square cloth lying on the floor in the middle of the room. I assumed they were going to cut me there, so I sank down to a sitting position and stretched out my right arm on top of the cloth.

Just as I stuck out my hand, I happened to glance up to the right and notice a young, good looking teenage boy sitting on the carpet against a wall. He looked like a Dagestani; he was too clean to have been at the outpost long. Our eyes met, and we stared at each other, expressionless, for a second or two.

The jihadis stood over me.

"*Nee nada*," one of them said—"that is not needed".

The militant had me get up, and they escorted me back to my room.

I was astonished, and I praised my Deliverer joyfully once the jihadis left me. I was not sure why they changed their minds. I figured it was because they were unable to find a vacant spot and a suitable place for chopping, or they did not have a hard enough surface, or perhaps they were simply testing my courage, since bravery was their highest value. It was a mystery, but it was an unforgettable moment, another miraculous moment, sitting with my arm extended, looking into the face of that innocent teen.

On the thirteenth day of the Marathon, the battle raged for my hand again. It was nighttime. It appeared as though the Hawks had won. Once more, I was ready to give up my hand. My door opened, and lo and behold it was Cap!

"Let's go," he said calmly.

I didn't often hear Cap arguing with the Hawks; he was under a lot of pressure to get the ransom money. Cap and a colleague led me to the third floor classroom. As we started up the stairs, I realized they wouldn't be chopping off my hand tonight. We went to the classroom and tried some phoning for the ransom money, but nothing worked out in Cap's attempt to call long distance.

Cap was frustrated with my organization and its inability to pay the big ransom.

"It really isn't a humanitarian organization," he said.

He berated me for saying my missionary group was a humanitarian aid entity. He equated "humanitarian aid" with a secular organization that had ties with the American government and, therefore, could readily produce funds. All Cap knew was his own culture, and in the former Soviet republics, there was a strong degree of government control and dominance. He did not want to hear that there were both religious organizations and secular organizations conducting humanitarian work.

"No, no . . . it's a private outfit, not connected to the government," I tried to explain to him.

Cap scoffed at the idea and shook his head. He just did not believe me.

"It cannot be humanitarian," he continued, "because it does spiritual work."

He always made affirmations, and I couldn't directly rebut Cap's comments without angering him. I waited for a better opportunity to speak. However, in his anger, Cap admitted that he hated the organization, not me.

Cap asked me if I minded waiting in my room at the outpost instead of waiting at the camp. It was a strange question, I thought. He knew I wanted to remain at the outpost, rather than be hauled off to Camp Awful.

"You're going to stay here," Cap said. "How do you feel about that?"

"Great," I replied.

"You will be a prisoner a long time while we keep waiting for the money," he said, before leading me back to the washroom. All the jihadis loved to use the word "*dolga*"—"a long time."

I rejoiced after this session, and praised God for His miraculous protection, though the hawkish ones still tried to get my hand every day for another week. God was keeping the wolves at bay, not allowing them to either cut or cart me to the camp. These marathon days were both trying and distressing, and I was constantly on my face praying to the Lord, pleading for my hand and my life.

XII

AVOIDING CAMP AWFUL

Herb

February-March, the Outpost

For some inexplicable reason, the Hawks seemed determined to cut off my hand before carrying out their plan to finish me off at the killing camp. My thought was that they wanted me to endure more physical punishment at the outpost, whereas once at the camp I could be killed too quickly and without that much suffering.

Peter, Debbie, and Philip came to my rescue every day. After three weeks, the Hawks desisted. Instead they focused on a new objective, taking me directly to the camp to kill me.

Peter and Debbie talked to the jihadis day and night, trying to persuade them not to haul me off to Camp Awful. From early in the morning until late at night, they verbally fought on my behalf. Every morning, while Bear was doing his morning water ritual in the room above mine, Peter would approach him, hoping Bear was in a good mood that day, and gingerly try to persuade him not to kill me. The sounds of their low voices, footsteps, and the splashing water drifted down into my room. I heard, and I prayed for Peter's courage and welfare.

While Peter was debating with Bear day after day, Philip was working on the other militants, one by one. Both Peter and Philip knew how to disagree with these jihadi soldiers, and they jawed with them constantly, sometimes on and off for nearly eighteen hours a day. There were always conversations and disagreements going on.

They spoke about the killing camp and what it was like.

"People die up there," Peter said to Bear.

"Yup – it's for killing," Bear replied, unconcerned.

They also talked a lot about me. Kicker once tried to persuade Philip that I was not genuine in my Christian faith and actions. Philip disagreed, and explained how, as an American, I could have my own religious views. Hassan had a notion that I was listening to their conversations and understanding what they were saying, but that I was pretending to be sympathetic about various aspects of their faith. He and Kicker were not convinced that I was sincerely interested.

--

One night, Nice and a couple other soldiers went through my room to speak with Maga, to encourage him in his newfound jihadi faith. I was surprised when Maga started trying to convince them not to send me to the killing camp.

"My friend faced the clubbing line there," Maga said. "He later died. It was not good."

Nice was noncommittal in his response and didn't say anything, but he knew Maga was right about how terrible running the gauntlet was.

After professing faith in radical Islam, Maga prayed five times a day at the set times. I listened to him praying on the other side of the door, talking to God quietly. Once, he mentioned my name—he was praying for me, asking God to spare me! I could hardly believe my ears. Maga and I had a special relationship, trapped together as we were at the outpost, even though we'd never met nor said a word to one another.

--

Bear truly seemed more like beast than man. He had no compassion for his victims. Peter repeatedly brought Bear, as the sergeant, to a point of decision for or against my being carted off, and Bear repeatedly said the dreaded "*yeździet*"—"riding to the killing camp." When I heard this word, pure fear would strike my heart, and I would intensely ask the Lord to frustrate their scheme.

Many times, they said this word, the horrible word. It was terrifying. Everything would be still and silent, except their voices. The jihadis were standing around debating.

"*On yeździet!*" someone would shout—he is riding! It was time for me to go to Camp Awful.

Bedlam would follow. My captors would scamper around, gathering supplies, preparing to leave. I would lie face down on the floor, desperately praying. I could sense angelic and demonic battles every time this call to go riding happened: it was a spiritual war, as well as a physical contest.

Several Scriptures spoke to me and helped greatly. A key verse for me was Psalm 44:4b: *Command victories for Jacob*. I compared myself to Jacob, being in extreme peril, wrestling with the Lord and fighting against these Esaus who wanted to tear me apart. I constantly asked the King of Kings to command four victories for me: that they would not cut off my hand; that they would not cart me off to the killing camp; that He would somehow solve the ransom issues; and that He would provide the pathway for my release from captivity.

I thought of Daniel in the lion's den, and Shadrach, Meshach, and Abednego in the fiery furnace.[44] Besides them, I remembered others whom God allowed to live after coming near to death: Hezekiah, Joseph, Job, Jonah, Jeremiah, Mordecai, and David. I knew that my God was the same one these men knew. He had spoken to Abraham,

---

44 The miracle of Shadrach, Meshach, and Abednego in defiance of King Nebuchadnezzar appears in the **Book of Daniel, Chapter 3.**

telling him He was his shield, so I repeatedly asked God to be my living shield.[45]

Many times, as the Marathon continued, I pleaded for the Lord to do the same for me that He did for the people of Judah in II Chronicles 20:22: *When they began singing and praising, the Lord set ambushes against the sons of Ammon, Moab and Mount Seir, who had come against Judah; so they were routed.* I urgently needed my warrior God to set ambushes and rout the conniving plans of the Hawks.

I desperately needed God to place an impenetrable wall between me and them, totally blocking their attempts at success. I needed God to provide more miracles—true acts of divine power. If He didn't keep acting boldly for me, I knew I would be finished.

Constantly, I praised the Lord and sang in a whisper directly to the Lord. Prayer had never before been so important! I had to admit a lack of prayer previously, knowing I had been busy for the Lord, but frequently not the prayer warrior I should have been. James 5:16b spurred me on in the solitude of my washroom: *The effective prayer of a righteous man can accomplish much.* Another verse that came to mind was Philippians 4:6: *Be anxious for nothing, but in everything by prayer and supplication with thanksgiving let your requests be made known to God.*

I confessed to God of being anxious in my predicament. I also realized how, for all these years, I had neglected the "with thanksgiving" aspect when asking for assistance, so I began to include this, my deep sense of gratitude, along with my pleas to Him.

Especially during the battles over my life, I sang praises to the King, thinking of the imprisonment of Paul and Silas in Philippi and how they sang and prayed and how the Lord delivered them.[46] I could not sing out loud, so I sang in whispers the few stanzas I could remember.

The promises of God were a mainstay for me. Jeremiah 32:27

45 **Genesis 15:1:** After this, the word of the Lord came to Abram in a vision: "Do not be afraid, Abram. I am your shield, your very great reward."

46 See the **Book of Acts**, Chapter 16: 25-28.

said it was not difficult for the Almighty to get me released: *Behold, I am the Lord, the God of all flesh; is anything too difficult for Me?* II Chronicles 16:9 told me that God would *strongly support those whose heart is completely His*, so I worked on getting my heart completely right with God. I gave all the challenges of my life over to Him.

Proverbs 21:1 was important: *The King's heart is like channels of water in the hand of the Lord; He turns it wherever He wishes.* My captors were the "kings," and the Lord could move their hearts toward my release—I constantly pled with Him to make this happen. Matthew 7:7 and 7:11 encouraged me to press on for an answer, because the Lord was good.[47] Isaiah 41:10 also helped me greatly: *Do not fear, for I am with you.... I will help you; surely I will uphold you with My righteous right hand.* It felt as if God was holding on to me, holding me above the dark waters of destruction, not letting me go.

--

As the weeks passed, more soldiers took up my side. The two groups, the Hawks and the Doves, became entrenched in their disagreement. Many of the captors I encountered from day to day, such as Cap and Ping, were Doves. They didn't want me to be hauled off and executed. Even K.A., though he initially liked to kick me, became more positive over the months and slowly turned into a Dove.

A small knot of jihadis were the most vocal Hawks: Bear, Kicker, Hassan, Abdullah and Muktá. Abdullah really wanted me dead. He reminded me of a stealthy black leopard: conniving and lethal. He would say things at my door describing how he would kill me. During the campaign for my hand, he did this often for the effect of purposely trying to terrify me.

"*Polne ruká!*" he'd say—"the whole hand."

Another one who despised me was Muktá. He would laugh whenever Philip tried to dissuade him about my possible death.

---

47 **Matthew, 7:7, 7:11**: The words of Jesus, Sermon on the Mount: "Ask and it will be given to you; seek and you will find; knock and the door will be opened to you.... If you, then, though you are evil, know how to give good gifts to your children, how much more will your Father in heaven have good gifts to those who ask him!"

He seemed to be a country fellow who thought in one-dimensional terms. "There's no need to bash his head in," Muktá once said. "Just shoot him with a rifle."

Muktá also suggested tying an anchor around my feet, taking me out on a boat into the lake near the killing camp and dropping me in to drown. He said this by my door so I could hear him, but I could also hear him when he spoke about my death with the other jihadis in their rooms yards away.

Muktá particularly wanted to see me dead. He had a driver's license. When the call to morning prayer came around before dawn, he would get up and go outside, start a jeep to warm it up and then honk the horn. He did this many mornings, trying to force the issue of transporting me to Camp Awful. Nobody responded, though. They knew what he was trying to do.

As I spent more time in the outpost, I discovered that there was a clear authority structure. The soldiers who held me were accountable to some higher officers. Several times, I heard these officers speaking on a closed-circuit television in the nearby TV room; they would give their instructions and reasons on why I should not be killed, yet. Still, Hawks like Muktá wanted to bypass the authorities, and they repeatedly tried to do so.[48]

--

There was a struggle in the outpost, and my life hung in the balance. I felt as if I were on the edge of a cliff, just about ready to be pushed off. I had a recurring vision of a precipice with gravel on it: I was close to the edge with one foot hanging over into the air. Or I was in a boat on stormy waters, on a dark sea of death about to engulf me. These turbulent waters were like the hearts of the Hawks, and

48 Who was at the very top of this kidnapping gang's chain of command remains unclear. Possibilities would include Osama bin Laden, along with Arbi Barayev. Herb mentioned hearing night time military activity in the distance and jihadis at the outpost going out to engage in firefights. These actions were not part of the Russian-Chechen wars but the undeclared civil war between Wahhabi fundamentalists and more traditional believing Islamists.

only the Lord could calm those hearts as he did the waters in the Sea of Galilee.

It was a challenge to fight against thinking about different ways of dying at the killing camp. I imagined pleading for my life at the bashing line, telling my murderers about my family. The thought of being thrown off a cliff kept coming into my head—I knew from Caucasus history that such killings happened to a lot of people. I could see myself on the edge with my captors urging me to jump.

Would I jump off or would I make them push me? Other despairing thoughts entered my mind: being shot with an automatic rifle; my throat being slit; getting a knife in my gut; being drowned; being decapitated. Romans 14:23 repeatedly helped me throw off these thoughts: *for whatever is not from faith is sin.*

The kidnapping killers reminded me of wild boars trying to gore me or of wolves trying to tear me to pieces. Bear seemed like a huge grizzly that held me in his paw with a vise-like grip. The jihadi Hawks were full of hate and determined to kill their victims, as some of them had done with the four beheaded engineers.

I did not believe the Lord wanted me sacrificed on the altar of their hate. My family was my little flock—each a precious little sheep—and my death would pierce their hearts. Why? Because of the cruelty and hatred of those who spurned Christ, disobeyed the King of Kings and were rebellious against His Spirit?

The whole situation seemed unjust and not at all according to God's righteous ways and words. I knew that no one loved me, humanly speaking, as my wife and kids, and I desperately didn't want to become only a memory to them. They were like pearls, and they would be deeply injured if I were killed.

Since being kidnapped, I had not wept about my situation. I never had the heart to weep about anyone or anything, neither my sins nor people trapped in darkness, even as a missionary year after year. But then the Holy Spirit convicted me of my unloving relationship with my sister that I'd had let fester for over thirty years. He showed me how I had been a Pharisee, not demonstrating the true kindness of Christ to her even though she didn't want to accept the Christ I loved. God opened the flood gates of my soul. I started to weep in sorrow and repentance. It was the beginning of many convictions and of much weeping.

The guard outside my door and the warriors in their rooms would hear me weeping, and they would pass the word around. It had an amazing effect on the Doves, spurring them on to argue on my behalf even more. It became one of the reasons they stated for sparing me: "*on plắket*"—"he cries."

These young jihadis, with their hunting knives and their rifles, fought so hard to act tough, but my unexpected weeping stopped them in their tracks. I wept day after day, and my weeping spoke to them more than my words.

Kicker and the other Hawks argued that I cried out of fear of the gauntlet line or because of the whole kidnapping experience. The Doves constantly maintained that I cried out of love for my family. I believed they all knew that my tears weren't from the fear of death because I had talked with them about being ready for heaven. Mine was a more unusual type of deep soulful sorrow and remorseful weeping that I don't know whether they understood its meaning. Only God knows for sure.

XIII

NO END TO THREATS

Herb

March-April, the Outpost

In March, Cap moved me into the bathroom where Maga had been, and he moved Maga into the little washroom. I briefly saw Maga as we passed each other—a quick glance at the side of his face. All I could note was his height: he was a short fellow.

The bathroom was much more pleasant than the dark washroom: it was roomier, a dozen mats were available for bedding, along with a nice long woman's coat. There was lots of sunlight. The walls were painted a light green. Six large prints of landscapes covered the windows on the outside wall; the prints were secured by strong wire mesh nailed firmly around the sides.

At the top where a slice of windows were left open, each measured about eight inches high by three feet wide. Light streamed through these small windows. It was a wonderful change.

The window sill was deep, and it was easy to stand on. If I stood on the sill, on tip toe, I could see over the pictures and look outside at a large section of the city and downstairs to the main entrance.

There was a road, actually a narrow paved street, in front of the outpost. Cars would roar by in either direction. The building across the street looked like it had been a store, but it was now vacant and run down. A lot of what I could see looked in bad repair, basically war torn. Once in a while, people walked past the outpost, along the farther side of the street – it made me wish I could also walk along freely. I wondered if they knew what was happening in this building.

Looking through the top of the windows was a bit risky because the soldiers guarding the front entrance could easily turn around and see me peering out. I didn't want to chance angering them, so I usually limited myself to looking through a head-level bullet hole in one of the prints. Cap showed me the spray of bullet holes when he brought me into the room.

"See this?" he said, pointing to them. "Don't try to escape or you might get shot."

Looking through that small hole, I had a view of the soldiers and cars down below. It didn't always work; on rainy days the window would be wet and blurred, but being able to see outside with the sky, trees, and birds was cheering to me.

Every morning, doves would coo outside, and other birds would chirp. In the washroom, the bird sounds had been much fainter; however, in the bathroom the birds sat right on the window sills. They had a calming effect on me, and I prayed to be able to hear Arizona birds again.

I also heard more street noises in the bathroom: cars going past, sometimes caravans of cars whizzing by while people fired weapons in celebration of a wedding or whatever. A Chechen tradition was for brides to be taken to their wedding ceremony by gun-toting friends of the groom. Occasionally, staccato automatic gunfire would echo around the city.

During these months, my hearing became very acute as I lay listening through the walls and doors, listening to the soldiers' comments, conversations, and plans.

One day, Cap came into the bathroom, acting friendly and curious.

"How do you know so much of what is happening?" he asked.

"I hear them," I said. "I can hear them."

I pointed upwards to the floor above, where Peter and Bear had their conversations.

Cap didn't react one way or another, though I knew it was an unusual phenomenon in his mind. He simply turned and walked out. I hoped it helped him understand that God was fighting for me.

All these months, I was shoeless, wearing only my sweat socks. Sometimes, when I wanted to dry out the sweat socks, I'd hang them up and wore my street socks. I never could wash anything, except one time in the bathroom. In this new room of light, I saw the dirt caked on my arms and feet for the first time. After finding a sliver of soap on the floor, I washed them with difficulty, noticing how my skin peeled. My skin was also more splotched and freckled than before.

On day 29 of the Marathon [March 27] Ping unexpectedly brought me a broken piece of mirror and a pair of scissors.

"Here," he said, kindly, "this will help you eat."

He held the mirror while I trimmed my moustache, which had really been in my way as I ate. Ping's thoughtfulness was refreshing.

About this time, a new jihadi named Abduljabar started helping serve food and guard the door. He was a Dove, though very intense for the cause of jihad. His attitude was friendly, and we'd chat regularly. I discovered that his father was German, and his mom was Chechen. Abduljabar was tall, with light brown hair and no beard. He was quite young. He asked me what my favorite pistol was and was surprised to hear I didn't have a favorite. He was also surprised to learn that I did not have a car back in Makhachkala.

Abduljabar generally avoided spiritual discussions with me, as he was young and didn't seem to know much, but he showed concern for my soul and even gave me a little explanation about hell.

"You know that candle you have?" he asked.

I glanced over at my dinner candle. The jihadis had given me some matches and this candle with instructions to light the candle only when I ate.

"Well, hell is ten thousand times hotter than that flame!"

"I know," I replied. "We believe in hell also. The *Injil* teaches about it."

"What's the *Injil*?"

"The Scriptures," I told him. He knew I believed in the Bible, since we had discussed the matter once before. As a Muslim, he should have known, too—the Koran acknowledged the gospels, the *Injil*, as true divine guidance.

Abduljabar didn't respond, but just left the room.

--

Mats were piled in the middle of the bathroom, toward the outside wall, about a yard from three nonfunctioning commodes that were covered over with plastic. I seldom sat on the mats, but sat instead on the floor, against the wall. I was here, on day 36 of the Marathon [April 3], when the bathroom door opened. Not knowing who it was going to be, I quickly put my face in the corner and covered myself with the coat for protection.

In walked Cap and Hassan, both acting crazy and mean. Hassan was carrying a pistol, and he pointed it at me with a wild expression on his face. Cap was displaying his cruel, bravado demeanor. He told me to sit up and take off my sock cap and the old coat, which I did, wondering what was going on.

Cap crouched down, got right in my face, and talked to me fiercely. He was very animated, trying to scare me.

"Who are you really?" he demanded.

I repeated what I already told him about my name, my organization, and where TEAM was located. I acted bewildered, hoping to show that I had already told them the truth.

"Aren't you really working for the FSB?" he asked, referring to the Russian Federal Security Agency.[49]

"No."

"Why did you go to Makhachkala?"

---

49 The Federal Security Service (FSB) of the Russian Federation came into existence in 1995, an agency whose predecessor was the KGB. Areas of responsibility included internal and border security, counterintelligence, and counter-terrorism activities.

"To help the people."

"Didn't you know it's wholly Islamic? What kind of fools do you think we are?"

Cap asked all the same questions he had asked before, and I repeated all the same answers. I could tell Cap was trying to scare a different story out of me, if I had one. He questioned me like he really thought it was possible I worked for the Russian government. The only other possibility was that I was telling the truth: I was there to love people.

Hassan stood behind Cap, a few feet away, pointing the gun at me. He didn't say anything.

Just as Cap was about to corner me with more questions, Abduljabar came to my rescue. He was temporarily the door guard, rather than Philip, and he didn't like them berating me. He stepped into the room and told Cap he had a phone call. Cap stopped his interrogation, swiftly slugged me on the forehead, and stormed out. It surprised and saddened me that Cap treated me this way. I had hoped that more of a bond had developed between us.

Hassan gave a powerful karate kick to my ribs, before following Cap out the door. This was the first extremely hard kick I'd gotten, and it really hurt, literally knocking the breath out of me. I winced and wheezed, curled over.

Abduljabar brought me a jar of water.

"Get some sleep," he said, trying to help. When he served me food, he would often tell me to sleep.

Hassan walked back into the room a couple minutes later, startling me. I was nervous, ready to get kicked again, and I flinched when he came closer.

"Don't be afraid," he said calmly. "I'm not going to hurt you."

He came in without his pistol and without the wild expression on his face. His attitude was totally different: peaceful and conciliatory.

"What are you doing now?" I asked. I didn't know what to think about this change.

"We have two types of talk," he explained. "One is fierce, and one is normal. Don't be afraid. I'm not going to kick you again."

Hassan seemed serious in trying to calm my fears; he wanted me to relax so we could talk. He started off the conversation by explaining why he kicked me. He said he had done so because of the abuse the Christian culture had given the Muslims in past centuries. My reply, which was news to him, was that there were no Christian Protestants as such before 1500, meaning they were not involved in any violence directed against Muslims before that time.

He talked about how great the Koran was. He explained why he believed in its perfection, and how, in his mind, its words lined up with scientific facts. Those facts were all the more impressive to him because Mohammad had been illiterate, having no way—outside of God's informing him—to have access to and write down these facts.

Hassan also asserted that the worst culprits and the main objects of jihadi wrath were the Jews—this point almost always came up whenever Hassan and others had religious conversations with me. In response, I carefully repeated that God loved not only the Jews, but all people.

Hassan listened to my comments thoughtfully.

"Why do Christians spread the gospel?" he asked.

"Jesus gave us instructions to do so," I said.

Abduljabar came into the room. He was trying to get Hassan to hurry because they had to take off for the local mosque.

"Are Christians supposed to be like their leader?" Hassan asked. He wanted to know if our goal was to be like Christ.

"Yes," I replied, nodding.

Hassan listened to my answer and walked out quietly.

Clearly, Hassan was dedicated to Islam and jihad, but he was also thinking about spiritual issues. God was working on his mind. I felt sure he had been pondering such matters ever since that early incident when they couldn't find my shoes to take me to the camp. I was happy that he was thinking and not just bullying me.

XIV

MUTILATION

Herb

April, the Outpost

Later, I discovered that the reason for my interrogation that day in early April was the U.S. bombing of Kosovo.[50] One argument I'd had up my sleeve for trying to survive was the idea of murder as immorality: God, through Moses, prohibited homicide, which was also a serious sin in the teachings of Allah. But Cap undermined my argument before I could articulate it when he complained that the Western governments could bomb populations, killing innocent women and children, and that was not considered murder. Yet, when the jihadis beheaded people like the four technicians, it *was* considered murder. I knew my argument was out the window.

About a week after the interrogation, Cap came into my room again. It was April 12, day 44 of the Marathon. He scrutinized the whole room, looking at the posters, the mats on the floor, the light coming through the windows. Then he looked over at me.

---

50 Between March 24 and June 10, 1999, during what has come to be called the Kosovo War, forces of the North Atlantic Treaty Organization (NATO) engaged in bombing operations to halt the wave of brutal "ethnic cleansing" actions between Christian Orthodox Serbs and Muslin Albanians in this contested region. United States war planes were among those included in NATO bombing activity. A few of the air strikes did result in the deaths of Albanians caught up in this maelstrom of existential war.

"Can you breathe well through your nose?" he asked.

"Yes," I told him.

He went out the door. Soon, he returned, bringing two other jihadis. As he came back in, Cap asked me, "Do you know why we're taking off this finger?"

He held up his right index finger in the air.

"No."

"Because you do not say 'Allah is one'."

Cap had explained to me that they might have to do something like cut off a finger. If they didn't, the Americans and Russians would not think they were serious. Cap was upbeat and rational when he explained this thinking, and I could understand their perspective. In the January video, they had threatened to cut off a hand or foot, so they had to do something. I knew losing a finger was incomparably better than having my whole hand or even my head cut off, so I was not as upset as I would have thought.

Holding up the right index finger was how the jihadis signified their doctrine of "God is one." Cap hated the Trinity, and taking this finger emphasized his point. Since I was left-handed, it would not be as debilitating for me, even though the right hand was considered the important, clean hand in Chechen culture. But Cap was left-handed, too; I wondered if he noticed that we shared this characteristic.

They prepared to cut me in my room. The two other militants moved sleeping mats out of the way and stacked them up against a wall. One dropped an army blanket over the pictures covering the windows, to conceal them. This same person had a camcorder. They were making the room as plain and empty looking as possible, so that no clues could be picked up by Russian or American authorities.

Cap brought in the items he needed for the cutting. He had another jihadi handcuff my left hand to a heater pipe running close to the wall. It was a couple of feet off the floor, about shoulder height from where I sat. Cap put a strip of rubber around the base of my right index finger. It was tight; after a few minutes, the finger became numb and white. Cap tried to cheer me up, actually saying things that made me laugh.

While I was sitting, waiting for them to cut, the fellow with the camcorder asked me how many kids and grandkids I had. He was a Chechen guy I hadn't seen before. His face was hostile, though his questions were more curious than unfriendly.

"Why are you here in an Islamic area?" he asked. "Have you read the Koran?"

"No . . ." I started to reply, but Cap interrupted our conversation. He announced the time had come to film the video.

Cap and his helper wore head coverings so the camcorder would not film their faces. The helper jihadi had been wearing his hood since he came into the room. His only job was to stand behind me and put his right hand over my mouth to keep me from yelling—they had told me not to yell. The helper muffled me securely; it was why Cap asked if I could breathe through my nose.

Cap pulled out his usual knife, a large sharp hunting knife, and within a few seconds two-thirds of my finger was gone. It did not hurt at first, because it had become so numb. Neither was there much blood.

Immediately after the cutting, they brought in a cooking pan filled with scalding paraffin wax. It was as clear and liquid as water. Cap grabbed hold of my hand and jammed the stump into the wax, which was scorching hot. I yanked my hand away. He had done too much, accidentally dipping all the way up to the knuckle. Cap tightened his hold and did it again, just briefly. He wanted to make sure my finger was cauterized.

They uncuffed me, and Cap helped me away from the heater. I felt faint, so he lifted me up and slowly led me to a spot against the wall where I could lean.

"Now, now," he said, holding onto and supporting me.

He was surprisingly empathetic. I was not trying to act stoic about anything and expressed the effects of the pain, grimacing and groaning. Trying to buck up my spirits, Cap scolded me for not being tough like the Russian soldiers. He then placed anti-infection medicine on the stump and put on a gauze dressing. They gave me a cup of water before they all left, leaving the room in disarray.

The mats were flopped over, out of the way. That they did not have the consideration to flop the bed mats back into place was perplexing to me. I called out for Abduljabar and asked him to put them back down for me. After he left, I sat on the mats, stunned and alone in the bathroom. I was shaken, but oddly calm while praying to God for endurance.

--

Cap and his camcording companion returned minutes later to film another appeal for money. I didn't know they would be coming back so soon, and it surprised me that I had to perform again. Cap instructed me regarding what to say: my situation was very serious, and more fingers would be taken off periodically if money did not come soon.

"Oh!" I exclaimed at the finger comment.

"Just say it, say it," he said dismissively, waving a hand. My thought was that he didn't want to cut off more fingers. It all seemed part of their strategy to get the ransom payment.[51]

Cap walked out and left me with the camcorder jihadi to film. I sat leaning against the wall, resting my bandaged hand on my leg in front of me.

"The situation is very serious," I said to the camcorder. "Today they cut off my finger because no one acted quickly in relation to

51 What Herb did not know at this time was that Mr. K, the chief Russian negotiator, had recently suffered a heart attack, and contact had been lost with the jihadi captors. Cutting off a portion of Herb's finger was a way to warn everyone on the Russian negotiating side that more progress was needed in coming up with a ransom payment—or Herb would continue to suffer through additional mutilations. The finger cutting message was clear: Pay up or else. Negotiations would begin again once Mr. K began to recover from his heart attack.

money. The situation is that without money, a lot of money, a finger will go each time at certain time periods. So the situation is very serious. My health is weak, and I'm in very, very somber straits, to tell you the truth."

Cap had forgotten to mention the $3.5 million in his instructions, so I asked for as much money as possible rather than giving that exact figure. A couple of days later, I was worried Cap would have Philip watch the tape and learn of the slip, so I decided to tell him.

"I made a mistake," I told Cap, the next time he came to see me. "I forgot to say the dollar figure in the video."

"It was a mistake," Cap admitted, but he wasn't angry, which shocked me.

I held up my bandaged stump.

"You did a good job," I said.

He chuckled. He really had performed the cutting process well: a swift cut at the joint, a quick twist, and it was done. Cap knew I was not bitter about losing my finger. In his mind, chopping off a finger turned out to be a good deal, because he could be a Dove, keeping me alive, and still be a jihadi, maintaining the extremist Muslim cause.

Pain came and went over the next few weeks, but it was not severe. The actual cutting experience was more fearful than painful. Cap would come in and check on the finger, and he could tell I did not hold the mutilation against him. Every day for the next two or three weeks, they put on a new dressing and medicine. Most of this time, Ping would appear in the bathroom. He would crush a white anti-infection tablet and pour the powder on the stump.

After putting on the initial dressings during those few weeks, they began changing the bandage every other day, or every few days, in the weapons room a couple of doors down the hall. This space was small, about four yards square. The brick floor was bare, except against the walls, which were lined with table-high weapon racks and piles of grenades. There were many automatic rifles, mortars, and shoulder rocket launchers. On one wall, to the right of the door, was a small wooden cabinet with a glass front that was filled with simple medical supplies.

I perceived, after the cutting, that the soldiers became more favorable toward me. They apparently trusted me enough to let me be around their weapons. Ping even joked with me one day, suggesting I pick up a rifle. He was explaining how they wanted more shoulder rocket launchers so they could bring down airplanes.

"This is why we need the money," he said, pointing at the racks, "to buy all these weapons."

He picked up a rifle and offered it to me.

"Here – take it," Ping said. He was in a happy mood.

"No," I replied, shaking my head and grinning in disbelief. "No, thank you."

I played the pacifist, wondering what on earth he was doing. Ping may have been trying, by letting me see and even touch the weapons, to get my thinking more aligned with theirs. They really wanted me to convert and become a jihadi.

--

Ping had to return to his village for a while to take care of some family matter. For three consecutive days, Hassan became my food server and would put on the clean dressings. God obviously worked it out so he and I could talk further. Within these few days, Hassan—the one who tried so hard to chop off my hand and kill me—became a Dove!

Hassan was not really "Hassan." He was from Lithuania and had joined the jihadis five years earlier, back in 1994 when Chechnya's war for independence broke out with Russia. He was only seventeen years old at that time, because he was now twenty-two. Hassan despised the Orthodox Church; most Lithuanians were either Catholics or Russian Orthodox.

I generally listened while Hassan spoke. He explained how the jihadis engaged in kidnapping because it was the most available avenue to obtain money for their cause. He filled my ears with talk about how wretched the Jews were, and how the jihadis detested the president of Dagestan who aligned himself with Russia. They were going to try to kill him, Hassan said.[52]

We talked about the Koran and spiritual issues. Hassan told me more about the scientific facts he admired, and how Jacques Cousteau's discoveries seemed to corroborate passages in the Koran. He compared these findings to Christianity, making statements like, "Islam is very scientific; Christianity is very unscientific."

I started to counter him on these assertions but decided to stay quiet and poker-faced. I didn't want to constantly respond or ask questions to the point of being antagonistic, even though he said some foolish things. Hassan might have been expecting more animosity or objections from me, because he was full of them himself. The jihadis all had a war-like mentality: everything was black or white.

Hassan also talked about martyrdom. Willingness to die for Allah was an important part of the jihad mentality.

"Why do you want to live rather than die?" he asked.

I knew that dying—going to be with the Lord—was far better than staying here, but I wanted to keep on living and working for Him, if He willed it. I also told Hassan, "I want to live because of my family and parents."

"It's just better to die," he declared. He physically portrayed getting shot and dying by grabbing his stomach and starting to fall to the ground. He had affirmed to me before that he wanted to die in battle, in order to go to Paradise. Death in a jihadi war, he said, was the only sure way to go to Paradise.

There was a noticeable difference in the way Hassan treated me by his bandage visit the third day. By this time, he had seen me

---

52 Dagestan's president at this time was Magomedali Magomedov (1930-2013). He served from 1992 to 2006 and was a political moderate who wanted to keep the Republic of Dagestan associated with the Russian Federation. If there were assassination attempts against him by more radical Muslims, none was successful..

over the months, had spoken with me, and had already experienced the lost shoes and attempts to chop off my hand. All these things already were playing on his mind, and now he was seeing me sit passively on the floor with my bandaged hand, just a peace-loving middle-aged Christian man with kids and grandkids.

--

For the next few days, a Chinese jihadi I hadn't met before came to dress my wound.

"It isn't pretty," I commented, as he unwrapped the stump.

"It's not our fault. It's Christianity's fault," he replied. He spoke automatically, without taking a second to ponder my comment.

The Chinese man started serving my food occasionally. He was cold and ruthless, obviously a resolute militant soldier, and he hated the Russians. He said there was going to be another war between Russia and Chechnya—I wondered if this were true.[53] The guy was eager to get into combat, and he was good at karate; he liked to jump and kick open my door, rather than open it by hand. Several times, when escorting me back to my room from the third floor classroom, this was how he opened the door for me.

I wasn't sure if the Chinese jihadi wanted me dead or not. He acted like a tough guy, a hardened soldier. As he was changing my dressing, he suggested what might happen if my finger got infected.

"If that gets infected," he said, "we'll cut off your hand." He used one hand to indicate a chopping motion at his other wrist.

"If that gets infected, we'll cut it off at the shoulder," he continued, moving the chopping demonstration up to his shoulder.

"When the warriors get shot up," he told me, "they just cut it off and put it in scalding wax." He implied it was a good, brave way to suffer for Allah. I didn't agree and was glad they used disinfectant on my wound.

---

53 The Second Chechen War against Russia started in 1999 and lasted ten years with brutal fighting characterizing both sides. The combatants on both sides were particularly merciless in their treatment of civilians. Russian forces finally prevailed, See the foreword for more information..

Besides Ping, my other primary wound dresser was Abduljabar. One day, he hustled me to the weapons room to change my bandages. They always moved me quickly so the Hawks wouldn't see me, because those guys kept itching to kill me if they ever had the chance. I walked in and sat down on my spot on the floor, in the middle of the room.

Abduljabar was his usual friendly self, but suddenly, unexpectedly, he whipped out his pistol and pointed the gun at my forehead.

"Do you want to die?" he asked, boldly. He tried to look mean, but he didn't seem capable of making any cruel expressions.

I flinched. "No," I said, turning my head to the side and closing my eyes.

He moved the pistol so that it pointed to the right of my head, just inches away, and pulled the trigger. There was silence; the safety catch was still on. As I had done many times before, I affirmed that I wanted to live, and he sheathed the weapon. He went on as normal, changing the dressing and said nothing else.

Abduljabar was trying to inculcate more respect and submission into me, to show me that there really wasn't much of a bond between us, either at his own or somebody else's instigation. Still, his behavior was surprising and also very disappointing because in my heart I had hoped we were starting to have a kind of friendship.

--

Beginning in April, drivers taking prisoners to the killing camp came for me relentlessly. These were jihadis who went around to the different kidnapping rings, picking up victims for the camp. We later learned that there were some seventy kidnapping rings, and the drivers went around to them to haul away prisoners who hadn't come up with ransoms or converted to Islam.

The drivers were hardened men, persistent, always putting on pressure or some kind of maneuver to pick up "the American." They would come for me ninety or a hundred times every 24 hours—every single day! They would roll up in front of the outpost, sometimes skidding to a stop, and honk. Constantly hearing their honking was unnerving. I asked Cap to try to stop them from honking, but he said he couldn't.

The Doves prevented the drivers from taking me away, giving different reasons why I shouldn't go.

"You don't want to kill a man who has a son," they said. "You don't want to take a man who weeps."

One driver became very irked because he had come to get me time after time without being able to haul me off. I could hear him debating with a Dove outside, near his car, getting angrier and more frustrated as the argument went on. He was unable to persuade the Dove to hand me over to him.

Finally, the driver blurted out the jihad battle cry, "Allah Akbar!"—God is great!

"*Nyet*," the Dove retorted, "*Allah Lyubóff*"—"No, God is love."

XV

COPING BACK HOME

Linda

April-May, Phoenix, Arizona

It was a Saturday, so everyone was at home when I arrived there from the grocery store. I gathered them all into the living room.

"What's going on?" Amy asked.

"Steve Edlin called me," I explained. "He's here in town, and he's on his way over. He said something happened, but daddy's still alive."

"Well, what is it?" She was suddenly alarmed.

"I don't know," I replied. "He just told me to get everyone together."

We sat around the room, anxiously wondering what Steve was going to tell us. He soon arrived, and greeted each of us before we all sat down to pray. Steve then looked over at me.

"The team in Russia received another video tape," he said, obviously trying to be gentle in delivering this news. "It shows them cutting off one of Herb's fingers."

We were horrified. What kind of people were these jihadis? It was one thing to hold a hostage and make them say frightening messages into a camera, but it was beyond being civilized to start dismembering them. Well, so much for the Stockholm Syndrome theory that sometimes makes captors have compassion on their captive after being together for some time.[54] The finger cutting gave a depth of reality to the situation from which we couldn't really hide. I started to cry.

"How did they do it?" I asked Steve. "What finger was it?"

"It was his right index finger," he said. "I don't know the details of how it was done, but they said the video shows Herb with his finger bandaged. He still looks to be in good shape."

"Dad's left handed," Amy noted. She also was crying.

"That's true," said Jason, "it could have been much worse."

We were all extremely relieved that it was only a finger. I knew from reading and hearing different stories about the Caucasus area that the cutting could have been a nose, ear, hand, foot, or even his head.

"Why did they do it?" Amy asked.

Steve was silent for a moment. He was quiet and conscientious; he always stopped to think before answering questions.

"Well, it's a part of hostage taking," he said. "They're trying to show that they are serious. They harm the hostage to make a statement, and also for shock value. It is perfectly understandable to react to that shock: to be feeling a sense of evil, and a sense of anger."

This development was distressing to all of us, because we had heard talk that Herb was supposed to be out by February or March. Now it was April, and his captors were cutting off fingers. What was going on over there?

It was a sad, scary, confusing time. We cried a little, read Scripture, and prayed a lot, and we were very thankful that Herb was still alive. But I did wonder: if the jihadis cut off one finger, what would keep them from cutting off a hand next time?

Not long after we heard about Herb's finger, I found out that the man negotiating had been hospitalized and was extremely ill—too sick to negotiate—and his inability to communicate with the captors

54 Herb's willingness to repeat what his captors demanded him to say on these taped messages might indicate growing feelings of respect and attachment toward his captors, but cutting off much of his finger suggests anything but total submission to the will of the captors who mutilated his hand..

might have been why Herb's finger was cut off. The good news was that the negotiator recovered and was up and at work again. I prayed all of the time for this man who was working to get Herb freed, though I hadn't met him when in Moscow five months earlier.

--

Several times, I had the opportunity to speak at Bible studies and meetings. I shared what God was doing in my life, what had happened with the kidnapping from the time Herb was abducted up to now. When I spoke at some places, other people would hear and would want me to speak at their church, but I was careful not to overburden myself.

Some said to me, "Don't speak now, it is too stressful." However, I wanted people to see God's strength in me before the outcome was known about Herb so that if he were released, they wouldn't think the Lord's strength in me was only because Herb had gained his freedom. I felt God's helping me in so many ways, and His presence wasn't just for me.

Every time I went out to speak, people who knew me were overwhelmed. They didn't expect to see me walking around and talking without anger. Even I couldn't believe how much the Holy Spirit was with me. The Spirit gave me strength when I needed His power, and I was blessed to be supported by the prayers of many people.

In May, I was asked to teach a women's Bible study on Ecclesiastes. I hadn't studied Ecclesiastes much and had always thought it seemed to be such a negative book.

"Can I teach on something else?" I asked the lady in charge.

"Well, no," she replied. "It needs to be on Ecclesiastes 3:1-15, in order to precede what will be taught next in the study."

"Okay," I said, and I began some serious study of the book.

When I read verse 3:11, I was intrigued: *He has made everything beautiful in its time.* Also, *He has put eternity in their hearts, except that no one can find out the work that God does from beginning to end.*

"Amazing," I thought. "God has made everything beautiful in its time. How so?" And it was so moving to remember that God had put eternity in our hearts.

Then I remembered Romans 5:3-4 and how it tells us that through tribulation God produces hope. I meditated on the two verses and came to a conclusion: in Jesus, we begin an eternal relationship with God, and even though we didn't know how God works everything, this relationship gives us eternal hope—the hope of heaven.[55]

Considering Ecclesiastes 3:11 and Romans 5:3-4, it seemed like God was saying that we could glory in tribulation because He would produce something beautiful in the end, on His time. In this fallen world we will experience much pain and heartache—disease, sickness, murder, kidnapping, abuse, and so on. But through the suffering of Jesus on the cross for our sins, we can live with hope beyond this life, an eternal hope; and the realization that in His time, He will make something beautiful out of all the things that now bring us so much pain.

In other words: heaven would be the banquet; this life was the appetizer. If we expect this life to be the banquet, we will always be disappointed, troubled and confused.

I pondered what would happen if I invited people to a banquet, and told them that it was going to be a great feast with piles of all their favorite food. They might put on nice clothes, the women might get their hair done, and perhaps some people wouldn't eat any lunch to save plenty of room for a huge dinner. Later, the guests would arrive at the banquet really hungry. What would they do if they came and found one big table with a small basket of Cheez-Its in the center?

"This is a banquet?" they would complain. "Cheez-Its? I don't even like Cheez-Its!"

But I would say, "No, this isn't the banquet—it's only the appetizer! The banquet is through those doors. In a few minutes, we'll all go in

---

55 **Romans 5: 3-4**:."Not only so, but we also glory in our sufferings, because we know that suffering produces perseverance; perseverance, character, and character, hope." Herb also gained strength from these same verses.

there for a marvelous dinner!" Everyone would calm down, perhaps munch on crackers, and later go happily into the banquet for the feast.

The Lord was reminding me that we live in a sin-sick world, and we'll be going through some really hard times. Difficulties, like the hatred in men's hearts, would negatively affect my life through Herb's kidnapping. Sickness would touch my life through our grandson Caleb's illness. Knowing this life was only the appetizer, the pain won't go on forever, that soon I'd be in heaven where the banquet would last forever. Our hope, our eternal hope, is in Jesus. Through Him, God will make everything beautiful in its time – in His time!

--

I repeatedly reminded myself that this life was just the appetizer, as our family struggled with Herb's captivity and other problems that arose during the passing months. May was especially challenging: Amy was struggling with Caleb's Fanconi anemia when she found out she was pregnant again.[56] We were all worried, afraid it might be another Fanconi baby. I was waiting in the front room of their doctor's office, sitting with Caleb, when my son-in-law Steve Glover came running out of the examination room.

"Mom!" he said. "Come in here!"

"Oh, no," I thought.

I stood up, got Caleb, and went in with fear and trembling. Amy was lying on a bed near the ultrasound machine.

"Show her," she said to the doctor.

The doctor pointed to the screen and said, "Baby A and Baby B."

Twins! They didn't have Fanconi anemia, either. Steve and Amy were elated. But the good news was tempered for Amy; she really wanted her dad to know she was pregnant.

In May, Jason was to have been married to his fiancée, Linda. Before Herb was captured, Jason asked him to be the best man at his wedding. Herb accepted gratefully. Now Jason faced a vexing

56 Fanconi anemia represents an inherited blood disorder that can cause all sorts of physical problems and, depending on abnormalities that develop, may lead to an early death. Such was the unfortunate situation for little Caleb.

dilemma: if he went ahead and got married and Herb was released later, would it make Herb feel sorry because Jason didn't wait in the hope that he'd be released? On the other hand, if Jason waited and Herb were killed, how happy would his wedding be?!

We went round and round, discussing it from every conceivable viewpoint. Even John Jackson and Steve Edlin put their opinions in the hopper. There were many options to work through, but all of us knew that it needed to be settled, for the sake of Jason and Linda. It was hard for them to be constantly on hold, unable to move on with their life together. After much discussing, Jason and Linda decided to postpone the wedding until September. Hopefully—surely surely!—and Herb would be free by then.

At this point, I realized the U.S. and Russian governments thought there was little chance Herb would be released because he was the first American the Chechen jihadis had ever captured—and they hated Americans—and because Herb was being held in Chechnya, where it was very difficult for the Russians to get to him.

Still, the two governments tried to help Herb. In mid-May, Russian President Boris Yeltsin fired Prime Minister Yevgeny Primakov and replaced him with a man named Sergei Stepashin, who had been in charge of solving problems in Chechnya when he headed Russia's police and security forces as Interior Minister. Primakov had no reason to be interested in what was going on there, but Stepashin did.[57]

I prayed he'd be more inclined to help Herb get released. Also, Bill Daniels called me to say that Vice President Al Gore had

57 Sergei Stepashin had developed various connections with leaders in Chechnya during and after the First Chechen War, including even speaking favorably about the growing presence of militant jihadis in the region. Shortly after his appointment as prime minister, he referred to kidnapping gangs in Chechnya as "scoundrels" who "publicly cut off fingers" and deserved death. Whether Stepashin had any influence on the negotiations that were taking place is not known. He lasted only three months as prime minister. In August Yeltsin removed him and appointed Vladimir Putin, to this office Putin officially replaced Yeltsin as the Russian Federation's president in May 2000.

written a letter to the new Russian Prime Minister, asking him to do everything possible for a safe release.[58]

--

June brought my birthday and our 28th wedding anniversary. It was hard to celebrate these events without Herb, especially knowing that his chances for survival might well be decreasing with each passing day.

Early in the month, TEAM flew me back to its home office near Chicago by myself, just to pray with me and encourage me. During all this time, people from TEAM also had flown out to pray with us in Arizona, including the director and his wife. Nearly every time someone came, Mary, the wife of our area director Dave Davis, sent Caleb little gifts, such as books and Curious George toys. During my trip this time, I stayed with Dave and Mary at their home.

This trip was quite different from my last visit. There was no news, no formal meeting, just a lot of meals and fellowship. The feeling at the home office had changed; the mood was uncertain and a bit resigned. Everybody's string was getting tauter the longer the captivity dragged on, and there were only so many days we could wake up in the morning expecting Herb to be released.

I realized then that Herb's captors hadn't just taken him captive, but also a family, a mission, two governments, many supporting churches, and thousands of people who were praying for his release. The whole experience was traumatic for TEAM. Although they weren't always sure what the best actions were to take, the organization really loved us and really cared and helped whenever possible. For all of us, God was teaching us about faith, perseverance, and eternal hope.

Dave was not as harried and overwhelmed as he was when I first spoke with him in Moscow. The extraordinary tasks that needed to be done had since become routine. I couldn't know everything that

58 At a G-7 summit meeting in Cologne, Germany, in mid-June 1999, President Bill Clinton spoke with Boris Yeltsin about hopefully bringing a positive resolution in regard to Herb's captivity.

Dave had been through, but I knew he carried a big load. I thought this about everyone, actually. God was bigger than all of us, but in these events, we each had our part to play.

Mary and I talked a lot while I was in their home. She told me what it was like seven months earlier when they heard of Herb's kidnapping: it was 6 a.m., and our team leader called their house. She answered and then held out the phone for Dave.

"It's for you," she told him. "A call from Moscow."

Dave took the phone and listened for a moment.

"Oh, no."

Mary started to worry about Dave's response. She told me that she thought the news must be about something worse than death because she'd seen Dave get news of a death before, and she didn't know what had taken place now to make him even more upset.

"What's going on?" she asked.

"Herb Gregg's been kidnapped," he said, shaking his head. "What in the world are we going to do?"

Dave said it was his nightmare come true. He had written TEAM's crisis policy. Still, he knew there were limitations on how much help the organization could provide.

"We could do everything right," he told Mary, sitting quietly in their house some months into the kidnapping, "but Herb could die anyway. . . . Ultimately, the outcome is in God's hands."

I told Dave that I knew he and others were doing their best and that I was praying for the Lord to give them complete wisdom and strength.

Everyone at TEAM was encouraging to me as they tried to shield me from the severity of the situation. Still, with days turning into weeks and then into months, it was becoming harder and harder to believe that Herb would soon be freed.

The embassy had stated to our mission that if the captivity went beyond six weeks, we would be in for a long haul in time, hopefully toward success. I knew the governments had a plan they were working on, but where was it going?

Exasperated, I asked John Jackson, "I know there's a Plan A, but Herb's still there. If Plan A doesn't work, is there a Plan B?"

"I don't know," he replied honestly.

Although I really wanted Herb back, I could see the outcome as good—and God as good—if the final outcome turned out either way, whether Herb lived or died. I felt like I was sitting on a fence: on one side was "released" and on the other was "not released" and home to glory. I was starting to tilt toward the "not released" side of the fence, thinking this was going to be God's will, His decision.

I flew back home to Arizona, wondering when this family crisis would ever end.

XVI

THE ELUSIVE POSSIBILIY OF RELEASE

Herb

April-May, the Outpost

Attitudes seemed to be changing at the outpost. April was a turning point. After the cutting, I perceived more favorable treatment toward me, and near the end of the month I began to hear bits and pieces of good news. Some of what I was hearing turned out to be a mirage.

On day 53 of the Marathon Against Death [April 21], the Chinese fellow was dressing my wound when Cap came into the room. He was in a pleasant mood. He stood over us as the bandaging was being changed.

"Some U.S. Congressman has volunteered the money," he said, "but it will take a little while to get here."

Cap spoke in a matter of fact way, but I could tell this report pleased him. However, for some reason, I did not fully understand what he had said in Russian, so I offered no reaction. I stared blankly, and Cap just left. The Chinese guy stayed straight-faced, as usual, doing his duty.

Later, when Ping brought in my big can of macaroni, he said, "There shouldn't be a problem with the money."

He smiled slightly. He had been hoping for me to get out.

"Surely the Congressman will give it," he said.[59]

Now I understood what Cap meant. Once Ping left the room, I literally jumped up and down for joy, and thanked God profusely. I was amazed and thrilled at the thought that the money might be coming from Congress.

Over a week went by, and then on day 62 [April 30]I heard the best news of all. Early in the morning, the killing camp drivers had already started to arrive. One of the young men in the outpost yelled out the window to a driver.

"*Yáshik pashól!*" he said—literally the "Christian is out of here!"

The decision had been made to release me! Every day, I was comforted by this thought and by hearing other phrases that meant the same thing. Still, the drivers didn't let up; they still came honking constantly. We were all caught up in an ongoing drama, and everyone—the Doves, the Hawks, and the drivers—was waiting to find out what would really happen to me.

More days passed with the pressure on me becoming less and less, and I seemed not to be on the cliff dangling for life but ready to fall off. The freedom train was rolling down the tracks well. I had not heard the dreaded "yézdet" but instead had been hearing the blessed word "*yédet*"—"freedom." Both words meant "to ride": one to death and one to life.

All of a sudden, I heard "On yézdet!"

Terror and desperation assaulted me again. Frantic pleas went up from me to the Almighty's throne. Everything was in turmoil outside my door, and the Hawks were beginning to have me carted

---

59 This news had no basis in fact. Most likely, the chief negotiator, Mr. K, had fabricated the story in the wake of the mutilation of Herb's finger, hoping that the imminent prospect of a ransom payment might save Herb from future violent acts against his body, even including the jihadis deciding to kill him.

away. Only after some intense and prolonged arguing with the Hawks was I saved.

What unsettled and disturbed me was that I had heard so many positive words. Then the situation abruptly reversed itself, and I was almost on my way to Camp Awful! I realized that I could not trust the words that had given me so much comfort and hope.

Back and forth, the messages kept changing. In fact, they did, several more times. The Hawks were playing their game, trying to force the leadership's hand to kill me. I called this phenomenon the "anti-matter train." It was like the freedom train was chugging along well but then derailed, and the invisible anti-matter train started racing in the opposite direction.

I knew the Hawks were trying to derail my freedom train; I could feel their hatred all around me. It was really frightening.

--

Several times during the Marathon, I was completely undone. Outside my door, the arguments and pressures were powerful. The Hawks seemed to have won, and my back was totally against the wall. I truly believed that I was as good as dead, though I still kept asking God for my life, and I made myself lift up holy hands, singing and praising Him. I struggled to keep praying, despite feeling as if I was just a millimeter from meeting death.

One night, the argument about moving me to the killing camp was going badly. I was sure the militants would haul me away. Their hearts were like black waters: turbulent and terrible. It reminded me of Peter walking on the water but then starting to sink as he looked at the winds and the waves.

I was looking at the dark waters, I could feel my heart sinking, and, finally, I gave up. I quit praising God and quit singing under my breath. I fully believed they were going to kill me. Waiting in my room—waiting for the inevitable—I laid down that night in complete despair and eventually fell asleep.

When I woke up the time was early, about 4 a.m. The outpost was dark and quiet; all was tranquil, like those waters calmed by the Lord. The Hawks had not come for me. I was still alive.

I could hear the Lord speaking to me: "You have such little faith."

He was so very right. I determined not to stop praising and thanking Him, no matter how desperate I felt. Even when I was really tempted to give up again, He continually strengthened me.

Scripture passages about having faith encouraged me and kept me going. I knew my faith was flimsy and that God wanted to strengthen me, just as Jesus was always teaching confidence to His disciples. I knew He wanted me to believe Him for deliverance from death, which would depend upon me asking Him to bolster my level of faith.

Hebrews 11:1 helped to buttress me: *Now faith is the assurance of things hoped for, the conviction of things not seen.* The sixth verse of this chapter also helped: *And without faith it is impossible to please Him, for he who comes to God must believe that He is and that He is a rewarder of those who seek Him.* I remembered Matthew 8:26, and 14:30-31, which said, *But seeing the wind, he became frightened, and beginning to sink, he cried out, "Lord, save me!" Immediately Jesus stretched out his hand and took hold of him, and said to him, "You of little faith, why did you doubt?"* This was me: "you of little faith." I asked God to help me believe, to walk on water, and to survive.

--

Sometime in May, a fellow named Dima joined the prisoners. He was a Russian Red Cross driver from the city of Ruona.[60] Soon after his arrival, Cap had me return to the washroom while Dima occupied the bathroom; Maga was moved to a room on the other side of the washroom sink's wall. I saw Dima when we switched. He didn't look Russian but like a big Chechen: tall and heavy with dark coloring and a beard.

When Cap moved me back into the washroom, he made some

60 Ruona at that time was a mid-sized city in Finland. Before then, Finland had long felt the harsh reality of Russian dominance.

comfortable changes for me. They moved in a couple more mats for me to sleep on, instead of the one thin lumpy mat I had available before. They also started including warm sweet tea in large glass jars when they brought my food. At this time in my captivity, this act seemed like an amazing gesture.

Cap went in and talked with Dima frequently in his first days. His attitude with Dima was different than it was with me. He was harder, more businesslike, perhaps because Dima was a Russian. When Dima professed his faith in Islam after a few weeks, Cap didn't believe him and none of the jihadis brought him extra water, as they had with Maga.

Dima didn't yet have to face the berating talks—these developed over time when no ransom money arrived to free him. But very shortly after being placed in the bathroom, Cap told Dima about the death camp and the clubbing line, the *ócherud.*

"*Ócherud*," Dima muttered repeatedly to himself, as he sat alone in the bathroom between Cap's frequent visits.

I knew that thinking about the gauntlet was terrifying to him, as it was for me. Over the months I had admitted to God that facing the *ócherud* was beyond my strength. This threat especially bothered me when the Hawks would stand outside my door, taunting me, saying, "*Pólnee ócherud*"—the full line of militant warriors, ready and eager to bash in my head.

On day 76 of the Marathon [May 14] , Abduljabar was not guarding at his position, and two or three of the Hawks tried to break the padlock and get to me. Once before this had happened, and the men were just bringing me food. But this time, I could tell the danger by their tone of voice. They were playing with the lock, clanking the metal against the door, and talking about finding a key. They tried some other key in the lock to see if it would open. This became a moment of stark desperation as I pled with God, my face on the mat. The flimsy washroom door was the only physical thing keeping me from their hatred and my death.

Noah's ark became an important image for me as I prayed for safety. I could see Noah's family feeding and caring for the animals: a picture of peace within the ark, while all around outside the weather was turbulent. The ark gave me great comfort. I imagined my little washroom—dark as the inside of the ark during the deluge must have been—to be the ark of protection, keeping me safe from the storm of fiends outside.

Another night, silent fear again engulfed me as I heard an argument right outside my door. I was sure they would take me to Camp Awful at any moment. I grabbed my dinner candle from its place against the wall and lit it. As quickly and quietly as possible, I tore the silky linings of the old women's coats into one-inch strips to make bandages, in case they beat me at the camp and bloodied me. I worked by candlelight, trying to mute the sound of tearing fabric, keeping an eye on the door. Once I had several strips in my pockets, I blew out the candle and put it, along with the matches, into a pocket. Then, I waited for the Hawks to come in and grab me.

But they did not get in—another miracle! Each evening, God kept these wolves at bay. I left the candle in my pocket, thinking I would have it if they took me to the camp. Waiting in my room, lying down night after night, the candle flattened out in my pocket.

The truth that gave me the most hope in the face of these threats was God's character. From all my years worshipping the Lord and studying His Word, I knew that He was compassionate, gracious, merciful, understanding, fatherly, and full of loving kindness and sympathy for His children. I felt that I could ask Him for release from my captivity because of these attributes. He did not have to respond to my pleas—and He would still have been righteous if I were to die. Regardless, His goodness and graciousness were boundless, so I did not hesitate to plead with Him for my physical deliverance.

God was the same one who extended life for Hezekiah, the righteous King of Judah, and He saved many of His Old Testament servants. Jesus saved and healed many when He was on earth. Even

Peter and Paul had been miraculously delivered from imprisonment and death.

I asked God, if death were not a part of His unchangeable plan at this time, to allow me to live and continue serving Him, as He had done with those servants of old. I knew He was not cruel and would not enjoy seeing me suffer and die. God was not capricious, and would not let me die unless absolutely necessary in His perfect, bedrock plan for my life.

--

Cap and Hassan were still hoping I would convert to their form of Islam. Despite the Hawks' efforts, I frequently heard words about my release. The freedom train continued to run, and their time to convert me was shortening. One day, Cap and Hassan took me out for a last-ditch effort to convince me. They came into my washroom and escorted me, without saying anything, to a small, empty room down the hall. It was an outside room, about the size of the weapons room, with windows along one wall.

I sat down on the floor, Indian style. Cap sat right in front of me, a couple yards away and to my left, and Hassan went across the room to rest his weight on the window sill. Their attitude was quite human, like normal people talking, instead of like captors browbeating their captive.

Cap was doing his usual pitch, basically rebuking me for holding onto the deity of Christ.

"On what do you base your hope?" he asked. He was somewhat aggravated that I had not yet changed my mind about Jesus.

"On the promises of God written by the apostles," I replied.

Cap scowled at me with frustration.

"You are like a horse with blinders on!" he said. "You're not seeing anything else outside of those blinders!"

I stared back mutely.

Hassan had been quiet much of this time, just sitting and listening.

At last, he asked me, "If you were to die today, are you afraid of the afterlife?"

I briefly pondered how to reply, and then decided to be totally transparent.

"I'm afraid of the pain of dying," I said, thinking of the Hawks talking about their gruesome ways of killing me, "but I'm not afraid of death itself. I'm ready for that."

Hassan stood up and rushed at me. He got down on the floor and in my face, practically nose to nose. With his face twisted and intense, he exploded, "If I would torture you the rest of my life, it would be *nothing* compared to hell!"

"I know," I said, as calmly and quickly as possible. "If I'm wrong, I'll be in deep trouble."

The conversation abruptly ended. I was grateful God had allowed me to say this to Cap and Hassan, as they could see I had total peace and did not believe I was wrong. They themselves were desperately working to avoid the flames of hell, not having God's peace about it.

I found great encouragement in the thought of God's glorious crown awaiting me, and I recalled a couple of verses. One was II Timothy 4:8, which said, *In the future there is laid up for me the crown of righteousness, which the Lord, the righteous Judge, will award to me on that day; and not only to me, but also to all who have loved His appearing*. Another was James 1:12: *Blessed is a man who perseveres under trial; for once he has been approved, he will receive the crown of life which the Lord has promised to those who love Him*. These words gave me the peace of mind about death that my jihadi captors did not have.

XVII

REGAINING FREEDOM

Herb

May-June, the Outpost and Beyond

I was in my usual spot in the washroom on day 100 of the Marathon [June 7], when I noticed that the padlock on the door to the bigger room was broken. I told Cap, and he came into my room after nightfall to remedy the situation and, for unknown reasons, to move me back into the bathroom and Dima to the washroom.

"The money's in Moscow," Cap announced, when he relocated me into the bathroom.

His comment was unsolicited—he didn't have to tell me—but we had developed a type of bond after talking together and working on the ransom for all these months. So he chose to share this exhilarating news with me. I had always tried to cooperate with him, and Cap appreciated my efforts. He was obviously pleased.

I was both amazed and thrilled. I joyfully reflected on God's sovereignty: the broken padlock brought Cap, who brought the good news. One of the first things Cap told me when I arrived at the outpost was that I wouldn't leave without a ransom paid. Though I did not really know if the money was in Moscow, who had sent it, or whether Cap would ever receive it, I knew the main reason—humanly speaking—that I was still alive month after month was because Cap and his kidnapping jihadis eagerly hoped for a big ransom payoff.

Later, Abduljabar brought in my dinner. As he leaned over to set it down on the floor, he whispered, "They're letting you go."

I looked up at him but couldn't respond. I could hardly believe it.

The program for my release was now in motion. The killing camp drivers didn't stop coming, and I was certain the Hawks would have loved to slit my throat if they could physically get to me. But the higher authorities in this kidnapping organization had ordered my release.

Bear was replaced as the outpost sergeant by a very pleasant and helpful man who served my food for a few days. He was a father himself and, therefore, was sympathetic to my plight as a father separated from his children. He seemed like a voice of sanity in the chaos of life at the outpost. He knew what the Hawks were up to, and his presence made it harder for them to drag me off to the camp.

--

I hoped to be able to say goodbye to Cap, Hassan, and Abduljabar. They stopped coming in regularly to speak with me. I had a new food server now: a young country guy who was nice and considerate, with a simple, quiet personality. I didn't give him a name.

Then, one evening, Cap walked into the bathroom to see me. I hadn't yet lit my candle for dinner, but I could see Cap's form in the dim light that entered the room through the windows. I sat on the mats, watching Cap walk toward me and kneel down on his haunches. He was an interesting person, I reflected. He had so many different sides: cagey, but personable; fiery, but humorous; cold, yet sympathetic. There was more depth to him than many of the other jihadis at the outpost.

"What exactly did you say on the last video?" he asked.

It took me by surprise, so I replied as best I could remember. Cap should have known by Philip's report, unless he didn't have Philip watch the last video. They had promptly sent the cassette off to Makhachkala. Cap must have trusted me enough to send it without first checking my words.

He listened to my description and nodded. He knew I was telling the truth.

"Are you tired?" he asked. "Do you want a rest?"

"Yeah," I said.

He pulled out his pistol quickly and pointed the weapon at me.

"When you die, then you can rest," he said. His face remained blank.

I was shocked—his action totally unexpected. I didn't respond.

"Why do you want to live?" he asked.

"My family," I replied, though Cap knew the answer already.

Even as he spoke, I believed his actions and words were an act. There was half-heartedness in his voice, and he held the gun in his hand as if a prop, an afterthought. He was just playing his role, the captor role, rather than showing any other feeling as I was about to be released. His playacting was strange, even disheartening to me.

"You never really pondered if Islam was the way of truth," Cap declared.

He spoke in a mildly berating way, but with gloom, like the wind was finally out of him. He had really wanted me to convert.

"I asked God every day to show me if I was mistaken to believe that Christianity was the one true way," I assured him.

In one of our many spiritual conversations, Cap had challenged me to pray this way, and I agreed. It was a way of showing him a degree of reasonableness and humility in the quest for truth. I didn't expect God to tell me anything different, but I had kept on praying as I promised and, obviously, God didn't respond!

The new food server popped into the room and put a bottle of water on the floor. Cap picked it up, placed it closer to me, and then left the room, holstering his gun as he went. As he passed through the washroom, I heard him tell Dima that I was leaving.

I was disappointed. Cap chose to act belligerent with me, after many times of not behaving that way—and even becoming friendly.

This was the third time a pistol had been pointed at my face; it seemed a sad way for Cap to say goodbye.

Immediately after Cap left, I started wondering why he asked me what I had said on the video. I realized that I forgot to tell him how I stated that other fingers would be periodically cut off if the ransom money did not appear soon. He had instructed me to say this right before filming, and I had complied. As I sat and thought about his query at this juncture, I wondered whether the Hawks were still determined to take off another finger, despite the assurance of a ransom payment.

--

Two or three days passed. One blessed morning, very early, I heard a captor from the outpost—one of the Doves—yell out to a driver. The drivers were still showing up, since they had their own program and agenda.

"He's leaving tomorrow," the Dove yelled. He used the Portuguese word for "tomorrow," "*amanhá,*" rather than the Russian "*záftra.*"

"Tomorrow," I thought—only one more day!

This news was elating. I could not believe my ears, and I decided *not* to believe it for fear of mental confusion and disillusionment. So I disregarded what I had heard but kept praying for my release and hoping that it would happen soon.

Yet more time passed. Day 124 of the Marathon rolled around [June 29]. I was back in the dark little washroom, where I had started my captivity at the outpost. About noon, when it was time for a meal, my food server came in, although he didn't have any food with him.

"Do you want to go home?" he asked, nonchalantly.

"Yes."

"Come with me," he said, grabbing my shoulder.

He opened the door and looked to the right, where the Hawks' rooms were located. Then he pulled me out of the washroom, and we ran together down the hall to the left and down the staircase. I noticed that neither Philip nor Abduljabar was sitting outside my door when we took off. Thankfully, I didn't see anyone else around inside the building, thankfully—the Hawks would have loved to have knifed me.

Downstairs, at the doorway, was a blue open bookcase holding some slippers. The food server plopped a couple of slippers on the floor for me to wear, and then he hustled me outside onto the muddy ground. A heavy rain had just occurred. The day was cloudy, gray, and the air was cool.

Awaiting me outside were two young men, each standing in front of two different cars. They were parked in a row, following the direction of the road, and each man was standing by the driver's door of his car. I assumed these were the release persons; everyone in the kidnapping industry seemed to have a specialized duty.

Off to the right, behind us and a little distance away, stood a group of about six jihadis, watching. They were Doves standing on the outpost property, though I didn't recognize any of them. Everyone in the building knew what was going on, as they had been dealing with me for so many months. These jihadis were here to watch the release, interested in witnessing the end of the long struggle between the Hawks and the Doves.

The drivers looked like Russians: they were thin, with close-cropped hair, wearing regular civilian clothes. The driver on the left was shorter than the one on the right.

"Do you want to go home?" he asked me cheerfully.

"Yes."

The taller driver was even more cheerful. He tried to ask my name in English, but it came out in German. I stared at him, so he tried again in Russian.

"What is your name?" he asked. "What is your father's name?"

I answered his questions, waiting for him to invite me into his car so we could leave.

"Well," the tall driver said, "go in." He signaled for me to go back into the outpost.

My food server had been standing and watching behind me. I turned around, and he walked me back into the outpost, deposited my muddy slippers at the door, and took me back to the washroom. He left, and I sat back down on the mat to pray, deeply disappointed and wondering if I would really be leaving.

The server soon returned with breakfast (a can of boiled macaroni), setting my can on the floor in front of me and delivering a can to Dima in the bathroom next door. As he walked by me, heading out to the hall, I stopped him.

"Do you think I am really going today?" I asked.

"Going where?"

"Home."

"Yeah," he said casually, before leaving again.

The food server seemed to be operating at another level of indifference, as if I were attending a picnic while getting ready to go home. There was nothing to do but eat my food and wait.

After a few minutes, he again returned, and the two of us reenacted our departure: looking for the Hawks, running downstairs, putting on slippers, and leaving the building. I walked alone out to where the cars had been, but now there was only one car—a totally different vehicle from before. There were a number of uniformed jihadis standing nearby that I didn't know. I glanced around, but didn't see the cheerful drivers or the group of Doves.

This time, they instructed me to get in. With no hesitation I hopped into the right back seat. The driver, the rifleman in the front seat, and the jihadi to my left all seemed to be part of the outpost gang. Our vehicle took off, and we drove away from the old school building.

As we rode along, the jihadi to my left, who was guarding me with his automatic rifle, asked, "You're not Muslim, are you?"

"No," I said.

"You're a Christian?"

"Yes."

The jihadi sneered. "You're just *kaffir*," he said—"a heathen." He was very hostile. I eyed his rifle and the knife on his belt but didn't react to his attitude.

"Do you know that we are mujahideen?"[61]

"Yes," I replied.

"You know we kill people, don't you?"

I misunderstood him, and thought he was talking only about himself.

"You have?" I asked. He looked too young to already be a killer.

He chuckled and said, "I personally wanted to slit your throat!"

The order had come down for my release, and this jihadi knew he could not touch me, though he wanted me to know how he felt.

It was a short drive. We rode through the city until we came to another paramilitary installation. This place had a large green metallic gate and a sentinel standing out front. The guard opened the gate for us, and we drove to a house inside a compound surrounded by high walls. Several other cars were present. A Mitsubishi SUV was full of more jihadis with a new driver and escorting riders with rifles. They were ready and waiting for me, so I got in, and we immediately left the compound.

I did not speak unless spoken to, although the militants in this vehicle were a little friendlier than in the last car. In fact, the rider in the front seat seemed to like me.

We stopped again on an open road outside of the city. Another Mitsubishi was waiting for us by the side of the road, and I climbed into it. Right in front of me, beside the driver, was the fellow in charge of transporting me: the tall, cheerful driver I met back at the outpost. He was cordial, full of smiles, and offered me a cigarette. I politely declined.

---

61 Mujahideen is a word for militant partisan soldiers devoted to fighting for their jihadist beliefs, most often against non-Muslins who do not recognize or accept any variation of their Islamic faith..

Sitting next to me was a man who I thought to be another jihadi. He was wearing a t-shirt and military pants, and looked pretty unkept. However, I was mistaken: the man's name was Sergei, and he was a Russian who also had been abducted.[62]

Our vehicle rolled quickly down the road, and we eventually passed a little building with a green flag saying "Chechnya" in white English letters. Shortly after this, we passed through a series of two checkpoints, though nobody stopped us. I thought we were in Dagestan, but it was actually Ingushetia, the republic on the western side of Chechnya.[63]

We rode on, and finally came to a compound that resembled a palace. The main building had obviously been an impressive residence sometime in the past.

Sergei and I were dropped off next to the gate, and the Mitsubishi drove away. The large gate opened, and we were ushered in by an elderly soldier who led us toward the once fine-looking house. We walked up a few steps and waited, standing on the tile porch. The elderly soldier gave us mineral water before he led us inside to the dining room.

A tall handsome man welcomed us; he was sitting at the head of the dining table.[64] I assumed he was one of the leaders of the kidnappers. Sergei and I sat down at the table, side by side, and soon a half dozen other men came into the room and joined us.

---

62 Sergei Medvedkov, a former Russian soccer player who had been held in captivity for around eleven months..

63 Ingushetia, the smallest in land size of the Russian client republics, lies contiguous to the western border of Chechnya. Ingushetia had been a part of Chechnya but separated in 1992 when Chechens committed themselves to pursuing independence from the Russian Federation.. Until recently, Ingushetia has offered its citizens little political stability and waves of crime, corruption, and kidnappings.

64 Possibly Vladimir Rushailo, who was then serving as the Interior Minister of the Federation of Russia (the MVD). This agency was in charge of law enforcement and directing interior ministry troops such as those accompanying Herb from Ingushetia to Moscow.

We feasted like kings. They had everything: fruits, vegetables, breads, meat. The food was wonderful, stupendous. They even had Coke to drink—that was such a treat. Sergei and I were both eating ravenously, but I was eating the fastest. The man at the head of the table became concerned.

"You should eat more slowly," he advised.

"I haven't had any fruits or vegetables for months," I replied, leaning over my plate of food. "They are delicious."

The men around the table were all very calm and positive. I wasn't sure who they were, but thought they must be connected to the Chechen leaders. They didn't introduce themselves or explain anything to me.

The head man asked a few questions about my captivity.

"Did they move you?"

"No," I said.

"You were in Chechnya the whole time?"

"Yes."

He acted surprised to hear me say this.

Another man at the table asked, "The men who held you were bandits?"

"No," I replied. Bandits were local warlords and ethnic mafia—they actually were responsible for a lot of kidnappings.

"Then Wahhabis?" he asked.[65]

"No," I said, shaking my head. The Wahhabis were Arab.

I described my captors: jihadis—holy warriors fighting for Islam and against the Russians—many of them were international. The man showed interest about my answer, but my impression was that he did not know much about what was going on in Chechnya.

While we were still sitting around the sumptuous lunch table, the men began asking Sergei questions. They started conversing rapidly in Russian, too fast for me to understand. It wasn't long

---

65 Actually, such warlords as Arbi Barayev and Shamil Basayev were influenced by Wahhabi beliefs, as were many of their non-Arab followers who had trained at the camps of radical Islamic leader Emir Khattab.

before the men stopped their questions and stepped out of the room for a moment. Sergei and I looked at each other and broke out in smiles. We were on our way home!

Within minutes of finishing lunch, one of the men walked over to us.

"The plane's here," he smiled. "It's time to go."

We walked outside and got into a small car. The guard beside me in the vehicle looked pure Russian. He was big and bulky with short blonde hair. I had never seen a more heavily armed soldier: he carried a machine gun and wore a vest full of armaments that resembled sticks of dynamite.

"What's your name?" I ventured to ask him.

"Yuri."

"How can you, a Russian, be in the Chechen army?" I asked. I was still confused about who was who in my release.

"No, no," Yuri explained, "I'm part of a Russian contingent escorting you back to Moscow."

What a joy to hear! I understood now that all the men with us were Russians. I had been worrying about how to renew my visa in Makhachkala, and had asked God to take care of the visa hassles when I was free again. Here I was, surrounded by Russian officials who could take me wherever I needed to go—God took care of the problem beautifully!

Finally, the time had arrived to fly to Moscow. After a quick trip to the landing strip, we boarded the plane and were off. It was a government plane, with three separate cabins inside. Sergei and I sat in the middle cabin with a young man from Ingushetia and a tall Russian stewardess who treated us like royalty. The Russian officials from the lunch table sat in the cabin toward the front. About a dozen commandos were in the cabin at the back of the plane, and the door to their cabin was left open.

After takeoff, they came into our cabin with a little cognac to offer us a celebration toast—Russians always loved to toast. The commandos were all big, and each carried a machine gun. They were really friendly, and they knew our escape represented a very happy occasion.

Sergei and I started talking with each other, and I discovered he had been held for eleven months, subsisting on some kind of mush. He had two other captives in his room, as opposed to my solitary confinement. Sergei had been a professional soccer player in Moscow until injuring a leg. He was visiting Ingushetia for a wedding, and his kidnappers grabbed him as he left the wedding area. He, too, did not know how or why he had been released.

The man who had been at the head of the lunch table walked back into our cabin and spoke with us cordially. He handed me his card: his name was Vladimir, and he was a top Russian police officer.

"When we were eating lunch," I told him, "I thought you were Chechen."

"Thank you," he replied. We all laughed.

The young Ingushetian in our cabin was Vladimir's assistant. Being from Ingushetia, he knew some pertinent facts. He told us where we had been and where the airport we left was located.

"Do you think there will be war between Chechnya and Russia?" I asked the young man. I knew things had not been going well, and the comment by the Chinese jihadi had made me curious.

"If developments continue as they have been," he said solemnly, "I think there will be another war."

The Russian military buildup was beginning again. It looked like the jihadis would be back at war before too long. I was sad to think that the fighting could become worse than before.

I had nothing with me except the clothes on my back, which were now filthy and wasting away, and my sock cap. Searching through my pockets, I pulled out my street socks. I enjoyed taking off my grimy sweat socks and tossing them, knowing I would never have to wear them again. I happily put on the thinner pair instead.

In another pocket, I found the candle I had been keeping with me, in case the Hawks took me to the killing camp. Several inches were burned down from the nights I had lit the candle during dinner, and it was now only a couple inches long and pressed completely flat.

Later, I reflected upon this image: the flattened candle. I realized that God also wanted to flatten my ego, self, and sin – everything that got in His way. During all these months of captivity, God had been flattening me, just like this candle. He had been flattening, and yet, magnificently reviving me.

The flight to Moscow was smooth. Every minute took me farther from the outpost and closer to my family. I was thrilled. I realized that I was truly riding to safety on the wings of ***God's*** victory!! I stretched out on the comfortable, divan-like seat, and enjoyed the happiest plane ride of my life.

XVIII

JOYFUL NEWS

Linda

June 29, Phoenix, Arizona

June 29 began like so many other days during the months of Herb's incarceration; it was a bright sunny morning, and I was alone in my room, curled up in bed.

I was in a deep sleep when my cell phone rang. There was no clock to check the time, but because of the sunlight coming through the windows, it seemed to be much later than 6 a.m.

"Hello!" I answered as brightly as I could, trying to sound as if I had been awake for a while.

It was Bill Daniels, calling from the State Department.

"Is this Linda or Amy?" he asked.

"It's Linda," I replied. "How are you, Bill?"

"I'm fine. I have some good news for you."

Bill sounded really excited, which was rare for him. But I was cautious: His last "good news" was when he called to tell me that Herb's head was not among those engineering victims found in Chechnya. Good news was somewhat relative with Bill.

"Oh, really? What is it?" I asked.

"Herb is out."

This was an odd thing to say. "Out of what?" I wondered. Out of his mind? Knocked out? I quickly thought through all the "out" phrases that I knew. It didn't instantly occur to me that Herb might be out of Chechnya. To safeguard me from the captors tricking me into talking with them, John Jackson, my liaison with the TEAM home office, was to call to let me know that Herb had been released. I knew this was really Bill—I had spoken with him so many times before—but I was confused by what he was trying to tell me.

"Out?" I asked. "What do you mean by 'out'?"

"I mean he's out," Bill said joyfully. "He's on a plane, he's on his way to Moscow right now!"

My heart stopped, and then leaped again. I finally understood what he meant: Herb was out of captivity and was skimming through the skies toward Moscow – a free man. *Herb was free!*

My body could scarcely contain the joy that surged through me. Every nerve was alive. This was an emotion equal to all the good happenings in my life, rolled into this brief moment--my salvation, my wedding, the birth of my children, every birthday and holiday I had ever had—the thrill all wrapped into one second in time!

I flew up out of the bed like in an act of levitation.

XIX

FREEDOM AT LAST

Herb and Linda

June-July, Moscow, London, and Home

We landed in Moscow late on the afternoon of June 29. As I stepped out of the plane, I noticed what a beautiful day it was--sunny and pleasant. James Collins, the U.S. Ambassador to Russia, was waiting at the airport, standing down on the tarmac with some other American and Russian officials. He approached me, shook my hand, and introduced himself, then nodded his head toward a group of journalists and cameras.

"It will be quick," he said. "They are just going to ask you a few questions, and we'll have you out of here shortly."

"Oh, okay." Seeing reporters certainly surprised me.

A tall lady in a striped dress had been waiting with the ambassador.

"I'm Laura Clerici," she said, smiling and shaking my hand. She was the Consul General. As we walked slowly toward the reporters, she explained that I would be occupying her quarters at the embassy.

Laura was a thoughtful and gracious hostess, and I learned that she had been trying to help me during my imprisonment. After we finished with the reporters and drove to the embassy, she allowed me to call Linda and the kids. We could only speak briefly, but it was wonderful to hear their voices again. I had been thinking and praying about them for such a long time I cried, listening to them chat so happily.

Linda explained, "They're going to fly me out to meet you in London. I'm leaving in a couple of hours, and we should be there tomorrow."

"Wonderful! Then I'll see you tomorrow."

"*Tomorrow . . .*" she said, sounding as if she couldn't quite believe it. "I'll see you tomorrow!"

The embassy apartment was very pleasant. It was roomy, big and bright, neat and well furnished. It was quite a change from where I had been, I noted, as I stood in the living room looking around. When we arrived, they gave me time to wash up. Laura supplied me with some different clothes: they were clean! They were the clothes that Linda had left in Moscow for me.

"What do you want to do with your old clothes?" Laura asked.

"Burn them!"

Being able to take a shower was almost unbelievable. Washing up was a real chore. I noticed that I couldn't get entirely clean, no matter how much soap I used. All the grime and dirt was not going to come off with just one shower. I scrubbed determinedly, watching the shower bottom fill up with soap and scum, but eventually I gave up on the notion of getting really clean.

Two consulate doctors came to the apartment to take the dressing off my hand, examine the stump, and put on a clean dressing.

"The cut's pretty crude," one said, looking at the stump, "but it was actually done fairly well, considering the crude conditions where you were."

The consulate also sent up a barber, and I got a delightful haircut and shave. The "Solzhenitsyn look" was over. The barber was a friendly and sensitive, pretty blue-eyed woman whose husband was an FBI agent. He was tall, well dressed, and personable. He came in to chat with me, and it was interesting to learn about where they were from in the States.[66] I also discovered that the FBI man had been working on my release, and that he met Linda at the embassy and went with her to their interview at the Moscow police station.

The barber, the FBI man's wife, was a Christian. She gave me a large old hardback Bible, knowing I had been without the Word all these months. I could not keep myself from weeping upon receiving the Bible.

While she was cutting my hair, and throughout the evening, various people came in and out of the apartment to greet me. We all gathered in the big living room, where Laura brought in some food. I met a man with the U.S. State Department who had been working on my behalf.[67] With him was a Russian translator who had been standing outside in the embassy compound when I first emerged from the car.

"You are a tough nut," he'd commented.

A few embassy Marines also came to say hello and to give me a medallion, an impressive Moscow embassy Marine medallion. They knew I had been in the Marines many years ago, and it was a special touch, showing real comradeship. The Marines handed me a couple of t-shirts, and offered to get me some shoes and a belt, since I did not have any.

Later in the evening, Phil Cantrell, my colleague from Moscow who had been the liaison representing TEAM during my kidnaping, and I had a terrific and tearful conversation. He was elated to see me. I didn't know all that he had done while I was being held, but I had a good idea. His was one of the phone numbers that Cap and I called. He was concerned now that some of our calls had not helped me in my dealings with the jihadis.

"I'm sorry if I ever did anything to irk them," he said. "Sometimes I got the feeling that my answers had the opposite effect of what I was hoping."

66 James Treacy, and referring to the state of Washington. Jeri Treacy was the very kind wife who gave Herb his haircut.

67 James Murphy, the regional security officer posted at the U. S. embassy.

"No, no," I tried to assure him that I understood what had happened. "Those guys play all sorts of games. Their calls, the anger, the ransom program – they're planned. It's all part of their strategy."

I told him about some of my experiences. I wanted to relieve him of any sense of responsibility, because I knew he had bent over backwards for my sake. He had come to the embassy constantly, trying to find out what was happening with the negotiations and to encourage the governments to do their best. He was TEAM's main contact in Moscow, and he was supposed to be the first to hear about my release.

That morning, Phil had had a meeting with embassy staff that suggested things weren't going well. Depressed, not wanting to send home more bad news, he turned off his phone for the whole day. But five minutes after he had left the embassy, news of my release came in, and the State Department couldn't reach him, so they had to call Bill Daniels instead.

Laura invited our team leader to stay the night in another bedroom of the apartment, since he would be escorting me to London the next day. It was a strange night: I could hardly sleep. I lay in the clean, comfortable bed, thankfully praying and thinking about my family.

We were bound for London in the morning. Early, before we left, an important Russian police officer interviewed me in the apartment. The FBI agent, the State Department employee, the Russian translator, and Laura sat in on the meeting. They asked for descriptions of places and people, trying to get as much factual information as they could. I supplied them with many facts and details while they took notes. The Russian officer was polite and affable, wishing me well at the conclusion of the talk.

On our way to the airport, we swung by the Marine quarters to pick up a pair of tennis shoes and a belt, and to have a group picture taken. The Marines were kind, respectful young men. I told them goodbye using the Marine Corps motto.

"*Semper fi.*" – Always faithful.

We flew to London on a commercial flight, which surprised me because I didn't have my passport or anything else with me. When we landed, a small woman who worked for the airport met us at the gate. She guided us along the corridors and around a corner to a spot where Linda was waiting for me.

Linda looked beautiful. Her hair was lovely—and that lipstick! She was wearing a real pretty bright pink lipstick. She was beaming, and her smile widened as I came closer.

"Hi, honey," she said.

I just smiled back and gave her a big hug.

Linda

I was grinning like a Cheshire cat..

The lady sitting beside me noticed. "You seem awfully excited," she said. "Do you have someone special waiting for you in Chicago?"

"I'm on my way to meet my husband in London. I haven't seen him since November."

"Oh, does he work there?"

Unable to contain my excitement, I told the woman about Herb's kidnapping, the months of captivity, and not knowing whether he would live or die. "And now," I chattered on, " he's finally been released!"

The woman was crying. "Oh, my goodness!" she said, a hand at her chest. "It sounds just like a movie!"

I gushed on and on about how powerful God was and how so many people had been praying for us. The flight passed quickly. As we walked off the plane in Chicago, the woman gave me a hug and wished me luck.

Some people from TEAM met me there. They were attentive and animated, and none of us could help grinning. Steve Edlin and another counselor from the mission named Dave Brown said they would be traveling with me on to London. They already had three color pictures of Herb: one of him getting off the plane in Moscow; a second one giving an interview to news reporters; and another riding in a big black car with his bandaged hand showing.

The first thing I thought when I saw Herb's pictures was that he was wearing the same clothes he had on when he was captured—and that he had played basketball for two hours before he had been captured. His hair was long, he had a full beard, he had lost a lot of weight, and I thought he looked like Solzhenitsyn. My heart leapt as I wondered again if Herb would be emotionally okay.

The pictures had been taken off the internet, along with an article. I began reading about the news conference and the questions they asked Herb. I got to a part where somebody asked him what he would say to his captors if he could send them a message. Herb's answer had been "That God really loves them." All of my concerns melted away, and I knew he'd be fine since he was able to respond to that question in that way.

I was too excited to do anything. On the flight to London, I couldn't eat or sleep. I spent the whole time ecstatically trying to imagine being with Herb again. I realized there might be an adjustment, as we'd been through so many experiences that had changed each of us over the past seven and a half months that we'd been apart. But I couldn't wait to share my months with Herb, and to hear about his experiences, regardless of how horrible they were.

When we arrived at Heathrow, a London-based FBI agent met us and told me that Herb would land soon.

"I've arranged for you to go behind the customs area to greet your husband," he explained. He glanced over at Steve and Dave. "However, only you and I can go."

"Oh, sure, that's no problem," Dave replied.

We all had something to drink while waiting for Herb's plane, and the FBI agent talked with Steve and Dave. I was glad they had come. Dave was a funny man, and his sense of humor relieved the tension. He was always cracking jokes, and quiet Steve was often the brunt of them. They made a very amusing pair. They had come to be supportive and to take care of our travel arrangements.

In no time at all, the agent and I were heading back to meet Herb. We stood waiting, listening to the entourage walk down the corridor. Over the tops of several partitions, I could see the heads of the taller men moving along. When they turned the corner and came toward me, I couldn't see Herb at first. I searched the people coming, and then I saw him. He came around the corner, flanked by our team leader and another man.

I felt like fainting. Herb was so thin! He had looked thin in the pictures but with his hair cut, I thought his neck looked like a chicken neck! He walked slightly bent over, and he looked like he was eighty years old. Then, I saw Herb's smile and I looked into his eyes: in them, I saw incredible peace and strength, joy and love. What I saw in his eyes reminded me of what I had known of God on the plane.

"He's been with the Lord for seven and a half months," I realized.

Everything was going to be okay.

Herb came toward me with a huge smile. There was a small private room where he and I could be alone before going out into the terminal where the press was waiting. The FBI man ushered us into the room and left for a few minutes. We had too much to say in such a short time, so we simply hugged and held each other until someone knocked on the door. We then went out, hand in hand.

Herb

As soon as we came out into the terminal, a few journalists flocked to us and started taking pictures and asking questions. We tried to ignore them at first. Linda introduced me to two men from our mission headquarters who had traveled with her to London and had been waiting for us in the terminal: Steve and Dave. I smiled and shook their hands, happy to see them, and purposely not looking at the reporters edging closer to us.

"Mr. Gregg!" The reporters tried to get my attention. "Mr. Gregg, how does it feel to be out? Mr. Gregg?"

Finally, I replied, "I feel extreme, extreme happiness."

We started to leave the airport, but they followed us. I turned to our Heathrow escort and asked, "Why can't the airport personnel help us completely avoid the media people?"

"We need to have good relations with the press," she said, apologizing.

"But the kidnappers want me to have a lot of publicity," I argued. Hassan had even told me to wave at him on TV. The journalists were polite as a group, and so I answered some of their questions, but our team leader pulled me away from them when I started answering too many.

Our colleagues, Linda and I all stayed at a five-star hotel in downtown London. The area and the pleasant surroundings seemed like paradise compared to what I existed in so recently. As we walked into the busy lobby, I looked around at the different groups of people sitting beneath antique artwork in clusters of chairs and couches.

"I hear someone speaking Russian," I told Linda.

She glanced around, listening to the babble of voices, and then shook her head. "I'm sure it's only your imagination," she said. "We're not in Russia anymore, we're in England. You don't have to worry."

Steve and Dave checked us into the hotel while Linda and I stood to the side, enjoying the beautiful marble lobby. It was hard to believe I was here, free from the outpost. I couldn't describe it other than to say it was wonderful. Linda was equally thrilled; she had a smile on her face that never left.

On our way up to the room, we walked past a small group of men who were sitting in very elegant chairs, speaking Russian!"

In the morning, my hearing was still so acute that I heard someone speaking Portuguese outside of our room. Linda listened for a moment, and she looked at me with some concern. "We're in London," she reminded me. "You're safe."

However, when we opened the door to go down for breakfast, in the hallway in front of our door were two maids standing by a big supply cart, waiting to clean our room. They were chatting in Portuguese.

Linda smiled at me and said, "I didn't hear *anyone* speaking out here, much less in Portuguese."

My hearing was still very acute. I wasn't nervous, but I was very aware of what was going on around me—there were heightened senses that remained from my time in the dark room. After a day together, Linda thought it was amazing that I really didn't have any sense of paranoia, despite everything that had happened.

--

We spent five delightful days in London. We soon discovered that the counselor Dave was very witty, with a great sense of humor, and we had an absolutely riotous time. I never laughed so much in my life. Everything was wonderful! I was free and physically well, though weak and with rubber band legs. A couple times, we rode on double-decker buses and had to scramble out quickly at stops. I would follow along, last in line, my legs quivering with all the use they were getting.

None of the others ever saw anyone eat as fast and furiously as they saw me eat in the hotel buffet. The first day when we went down to breakfast, I eagerly explored the tables full of fruit, rolls, cereal, pancakes, eggs, bacon—all my favorite foods—and I loaded up five plates with food. When I deposited my load back at the table, everyone gasped.

"Herb, no! You're going to be sick!"

"Oh, I'm not going to be sick," I said, salivating over my plates of food.

I ate everything and enjoyed every bite. I had lost nearly forty pounds in captivity, eating basically stale bread and boiled macaroni. For the next thirty days, I gained about a pound a day until I was back to my normal weight, but I never had trouble eating great quantities of food. It was all so delicious. I would eat my meal and then ate the rest of Linda's and anyone else that still had food on their plate! The others sat back and watched me eat, laughing about the piles of food.

An organization called Inter-Health conducted my debriefing sessions. Two psychologists asked some mental health questions over three or four meetings, and a doctor did an exam along with some blood work. He was amazed when the blood results came back, since none of the tests came out lower than low-normal; even my iron levels were okay. He was expecting severe deficiencies, but the results showed that, even in difficult places, God had the power to physically sustain a body.

The nurse changed my finger bandage a couple times, and the doctor briefly examined the stump.

"I've never seen anything so barbaric," he said.

Linda leaned over to look at it, and observed, "Yeah, it looks like a burned cigar butt."

The doctor laughed. "Well, the hot wax has done a good job of keeping it from infection, but you'll need to have surgery when you return to the States."

I nodded. TEAM had already made plans for my medical care.

The rest of our time in London was interspersed with happy jaunts, by foot or by car, to places around the city. Steve had lived in London several years before, and he guided us around. On our last day, he rented a car and we drove out of town to find a peaceful, quiet country area. We stopped by a castle, and I found a new Day-Timer to replace the one I lost with my sports bag. At last, we found ourselves by a beautiful green lawn with big trees everywhere. It was serene. Then, we noticed that the buildings behind us had high walls with barbed wire on the top.

"Oh, look!" Dave said. "We drove way out here so Herb could recover from his captivity by relaxing next to a prison!"

We all laughed about the irony, but we stayed anyway, lying down on the grass underneath the trees, relaxing, talking, and thanking our dear Savior.

While we were in London, our area director Dave flew to Moscow to help the team wrap up their work with the governments. They met with the U.S. embassy and the FBI, and they wrote letters of thanks to all the Russian officials—everyone who tried to help free me.

Dave Davis and another colleague were even able to meet briefly with the negotiator, Mr. K: he was a big and brawny man, businesslike, and a little cocky. They talked for an hour in a smoky, noisy hotel, and Dave gave the man a gift of thanks for all his hard work on our behalf. The word was, no ransom was paid – no money from Congress—but the negotiator wouldn't reveal what had happened to get me released.

"It was a risk for me and for those of us who live here," the negotiator said. "I'm glad I did it, and that it all turned out well, but you'll probably never see me again."

The Russian and American governments were delighted that things turned out so well. Everybody was pleased. At the TEAM home office, everyone stopped their work, went down to the chapel, sang enthusiastically and praised the Lord. People all over the world rejoiced in our powerful God, and each of us was able to see the effect of united, committed prayer. My release came from the prayers of thousands of people—the whole outpost experience truly had been an enormous spiritual battle.

Linda

Herb and I could not sleep for excitement. Each evening we stayed up late, talking and sharing what happened in each of our lives from the time Herb left the orphanage and through all our days of captivity. He was like a fountain, gushing stories about the outpost. I described my vision experience on the airplane and what was going on back home. We were so greatly blessed to be together again.

As we finished relating everything that had happened in our lives, one thing became overwhelmingly obvious: God had taken such good care of both of us. Though Herb had been held captive—though all of us had, in a way, also been held captive – he believed that the young men at the outpost were the true captives.

"They are enmeshed in this huge evil machine," Herb said. "But, despite themselves, the love of Christ was really attractive to them—it's something their hearts haven't encountered before in their violent form of religion. Some of those young guys still have a heart that's touchable, a heart that hungers. I'm convinced that's one reason why God had this happen: to touch some of them."

"Do you think any of them would turn to Christ?" I asked. "I certainly hope so," Herb replied. "God was working in them. I hope they can escape from the grasp of jihad, though it may be at the cost of their lives."

Seeing how Herb had absolutely no bitterness or anger, only compassion toward his captors, something wonderful occurred to me. It was like the days of Shadrach, Meshach and Abednego: they had been in the fiery furnace, but Jesus was with them, and they didn't get burned and they didn't smell like smoke.

I looked at my husband, and realized that he also had been in the fiery furnace, and that Jesus had been with him. Therefore, he also didn't get burned and he didn't even smell like smoke. In spite of the desperate, extended time of abuse and deprivation, God had held Herb's emotions and soul in His own mighty hands and kept him from all harm.

XX

SOME REFLECTIONS

Herb

July 1999 and Beyond

Linda and I landed back in Arizona late in the first week of July. The ordeal was over. I was a free man, as in Psalm 124: *Our soul has escaped as a bird out of the snare of the trapper; the snare is broken, and we have escaped.*

TEAM had me visit a counselor, but after a few sessions the counselor agreed with me that it was not necessary. I have never had a flashback, nightmare, or any other trauma from the captivity.

Actually, after I related my story to the counselor, he asked me to share it with his church and with some city officials. Many times, I was able to speak at churches and other places to share the story of God's grace and faithfulness.

Looking back at my time in captivity, I could see that the Lord wanted to revolutionize my life, in order to know Him better and to help others know Him better. He wanted to show His *power, goodness, compassion, grace, presence, righteousness, and victory* to me and to others. He allowed me to suffer for Him, and He wanted me to be a witness for Him to those young jihadis in Chechnya, whom I had not even thought about or prayed for during my time in Dagestan.

No, I hadn't, but God had, and He loved them. So He plunked me down in the middle of them to be an example of a follower of Christ who would die before denying Him. This message spoke to those jihadis who constantly faced death for their religious war. They came from all over the world and were willing to die for their misguided cause. But we have the greatest cause because we have Christ.

The Lord used my kidnapping to drive home the point that Jesus called us to carry our cross and follow Him, and that the gospel was not without cost. Timur later explained how the gospel became more precious to the church in Dagestan, because they realized the price people paid to share God's perfect Word with them – and this gave them more courage to stand firm and to be living examples in that rough and antagonistic atmosphere.

Now they had to worship so much on their own, since the kidnapping ended our presence and work in Dagestan. All missionaries in the region at that time had to leave, and the Russian government forbade any foreigners to go back. Linda and I especially could not return, so we moved on to another place of ministry.[68]

God used the experience of my captivity to make me more Christ-like. He used His Holy Spirit to convict and prune me of many sin patterns in order to make me more patient, loving, faithful, prayerful, and kind. He wanted me to realize my weakness so I would rely on Him for my strength, as He told Paul, "*My power is perfected in weakness.*"[69]

My captivity was not a time of condemnation, but an amazingly alive time of spiritual revival! Coming home has been a challenge to live according to that same standard, but I strive each day to follow the victorious, obedient life God showed me in that small washroom. I remind myself of Psalm 56:13: *For You have delivered my soul from death, indeed my feet from stumbling, so that I may walk before God in the light of the living.*

---

68 The next missionary assignments took Herb and Linda to China and Mexico, as described in the Afterword that follows.

69 See **II Corinthians, 12: 9.**

AFTERWORD: 231 DAYS

Herb and Linda were safely back home in Arizona by mid-July 1999. Less than a month later they received news about a major Chechen military incursion into Dagestan. A Chechen warlord named Shamil Basayev (1965-2006), along with Muslim fundamentalist Emir Khattab, trained and led this force of 1,400 followers, known as the Islamic International Brigade, into northern Dagestan.[70] Their invasion turned out to be a futile effort to bring into being a Chechen-Dagestani Islamist republic with no ties to the Russian Federation. In response, Kremlin leaders, prominent among them the rising star Vladimir Putin, used this Wahhabi-inspired action to invade Chechnya anew in what became the more than bloody Second Chechen War (1999-2009) that cost at least 60,000 combatant and civilian lives.[71]

---

70 Basayev remains a mysterious figure who supposedly hated the Russians but was also accused of working with them when convenient. He was known to engage in kidnapping and had associations with Arbi Barayev. Russian leaders believed him to be involved in the November 2002 Moscow Theater attack that killed more than 100 civilian hostages. On a most wanted list, a Russian drone strike ended his life in July 2006. As noted above, Khattab died in 2002 from exposure to a poison letter.

71 By 1999 Putin had risen to the post of First Premier or second in command of the Russian Federation. Boris Yeltsin had supported Putin's ascendance. Putin in turn helped undercut Yeltsin by pointing to the latter's willingness to agree to Chechnya's independence. When Yeltsin resigned in late 1999 amid alleged scandals and reported poor health,, Putin rose to the post of Acting President and then President of the Federation. Part of his appeal was his determined stand to bring Chechnya back into the Russian fold through backbreaking defeats in the Second Chechen War. Doing so fit into Putin's long-term objective of recreating the U.S.S.R., in essence having Russia become again the world power that it once was before its 1991 collapse.

So went war-related events in the North Caucasus region. Finally, in 2009 Chechnya gave up its pretensions to function as an independent nation and reverted to its former status as a Soviet-dominated republic, now included in the Russian Federation. Economic corruption, widespread criminal activity, and political violence have continued there over time, even though many of the warlords and political leaders of the 1990s had long since met violent deaths.

Dagestan was only slightly more stable but still suffered from high unemployment, street crime, acts of violence, and many moments of political instability. One can only wonder how much better life would have been for the people living there had the TEAM missionaries been able to get a solid Christian foothold in this unstable area of the world.

Herb and Linda, meanwhile, took less than a year to rest and recover from their ordeal. During this time they each wrote their personal memoirs which form the basis of this text. At no point did they doubt or neglect their devoted Christian worship of God and His son Jesus Christ. During this reflective interlude, they formulated plans to continue their missionary outreach activities under the auspices TEAM and its affiliated churches.

In 2000 doors opened for them to travel to China. They first located in Harbin, a provincial city in northeast China with a population then approaching ten million people. Three years later they moved to Xining in western China. Their focus in both locations was not on church planting, rather on evangelism outreach directed toward those living around them, almost all of whom knew little or nothing about God's redeeming grace. In Xining, an industrial city of about two million residents and with strong Muslim and Buddhist ties, Herb and Linda concentrated on witnessing to and working with Tibetan students enrolled in colleges there.

Linda had earlier developed multiple sclerosis, and her leg went numb during the spring of 2007. They moved back to Arizona praying that Linda's leg would get strong enough to resume their foreign

So went war-related events in the North Caucasus region. Finally, in 2009 Chechnya gave up its pretensions to function as an independent nation and reverted to its former status as a Soviet-dominated republic, now included in the Russian Federation. Economic corruption, widespread criminal activity, and political violence have continued there over time, even though many of the warlords and political leaders of the 1990s had long since met violent deaths.

Dagestan was only slightly more stable but still suffered from high unemployment, street crime, acts of violence, and many moments of political instability. One can only wonder how much better life would have been for the people living there had the TEAM missionaries been able to get a solid Christian foothold in this unstable area of the world.

Herb and Linda, meanwhile, took less than a year to rest and recover from their ordeal. During this time they each wrote their personal memoirs which form the basis of this text. At no point did they doubt or neglect their devoted Christian worship of God and His son Jesus Christ. During this reflective interlude, they formulated plans to continue their missionary outreach activities under the auspices TEAM and its affiliated churches.

In 2000 doors opened for them to travel to China. They first located in Harbin, a provincial city in northeast China with a population then approaching ten million people. Three years later they moved to Xining in western China. Their focus in both locations was not on church planting, rather on evangelism outreach directed toward those living around them, almost all of whom knew little or nothing about God's redeeming grace. In Xining, an industrial city of about two million residents and with strong Muslim and Buddhist ties, Herb and Linda concentrated on witnessing to and working with Tibetan students enrolled in colleges there.

Linda had earlier developed multiple sclerosis, and her leg went numb during the spring of 2007. They moved back to Arizona praying that Linda's leg would get strong enough to resume their foreign missions calling. Exceptionally good news followed, and her leg regained enough strength for them to move to Guadalajara, Mexico, in June 2008. There they launched a new church-building ministry aimed at those not yet reached with God's Word in the middle and upper business class. Herb and Linda organized a small cell group that actively studied the Bible, discovering God's love for them through the death and resurrection of Jesus. They learned to love and trust the Scriptures for direction and truth. They shared their newfound faith with other neighbors, and so the fellowship grew. Three other colleagues also started neighborhood Bible study and fellowship groups. These small worship groups then began meeting together once a month in what was an abundantly blessed ministry of pioneer church planting.

After five years in Guadalajara, Herb and Linda decided to retire from TEAM and their active foreign missionary work. They relocated to Oregon where they settled close to their daughter Amy, her husband Steve, and their grandchildren. Finally, after being overseas for so many years, Herb and Linda are able to experience the joy of sharing in the lives of their grandchildren.

At the same time, they have remained active in their Christian witness. Herb even enrolled in a class at Mount Hood Community College so he could share his believing faith with younger students. He and Linda have also led a Navigator club on that campus. This activity had a positive result in helping students to further develop and stay strong in their faith. More recently they have been mentoring a group of young adult Christians who want to live out the Great Commission of Matthew.

Just as Herb prayed for the welfare of his jihadi captors after regaining his freedom, he and Linda have kept praying for the non-believing souls living around them. They rejoice in seeing people transition from a world of spiritual darkness as they are born again in the marvelous light and life of Jesus Christ. As true saints, they have and still are reaching up to God as He has reached down to

Acknowledgments

High among those who deserve my grateful thanks are two of my Hollywood-based associates, Bob Burris and Phil Hurn. They introduced me to this miraculous story about the courageous believing faith of missionary Herb Gregg. Through Bob and Phil, I made contact with Herb and his remarkable wife Linda. We communicated through video conference calls and email messages as the Greggs explained the details of what had happened to them.

Just as important, Herb and Linda shared with me the written memoirs they had composed once back in America after Herb's release from captivity. My purpose has been to blend their stories into a narrative whole as they revealed their experiences before, during, and after those trying 231 days of faith and hope involving Herb's survival and release from captivity.

My wife, Karen W. Martin, helped me develop the overall story line as revealed through the overlapping thoughts and feelings of Herb and Linda. Karen also assisted me in doing background historical research about the North Caucasus region, especially Dagestan and Chechnya; and she also took the lead in identifying scriptural passages, drawn from the standard NIV translation, that are included in the footnotes—those not specially spelled out in the text by Herb and Linda.

Two individuals who directly participated in this story were especially helpful in providing valuable information about key events. James Treacy, the FBI agent (Assistant Legal Attaché) then assigned to the American embassy in Moscow, offered me many insights, especially in regard to the role of Russian officials involved in the efforts to liberate Herb. Christine Rasulov-Hartju, Linda's youthful TEAM companion, helped me better understand how she and Linda initially coped with the news of Herb's abduction.

A number of special encouragers in my own church family offered valuable guidance and sage advice along the way. My debt is great to Pastor Duane Brooks, Missions and Evangelism Pastor Jeremy Scott, and Chapel Class Connect Group leaders Earl and Janet Nichols. Those who graciously read and commented on an earlier version of the manuscript include David and Karen Batchelor and Richard and Mary Lynn Hollis. Brian McClain made useful suggestions in developing the map that appears at the beginning of this volume.

Two other readers deserve special mention. I have known Sara Allen Shook since my grade school days back in northern Ohio. Her comments were most helpful in bringing clarity to the story line, as were those of our daughter Joelle Kathryn Martin Hussey. Terri Stucky, formerly with TEAM, was a generous source of information about this incredible missionary organization. Also very encouraging were my California-based contacts Rachel Tash and Joe Gallagher, along with James Hart, my Pittsburgh friend whose support I will ever cherish in his determination to see this story come alive in book form.

Brian Rouff, managing partner of Imagine Communications, has performed yeoman service in moving the manuscript through the publication process. He has been an invaluable partner all along the way. Besides Brian, I would like to thank Lucy Holtsnider, whose professional design talents greatly elevated the internal and external look and feel of this book.

In closing, let me also mention that an hour-long documentary film, also titled *231 Days*, is available as a companion work to this volume. It features Herb and Linda, along with their two children,

Jason and Amy, in dramatically explaining the God-breathed miracle of Herb's survival and rescue despite what seemed like impossible human odds.

--JKM

Printed in the USA
CPSIA information can be obtained
at www.ICGtesting.com
LVHW052127300823
756812LV00038B/1303

9 798987 897409